Bloom's

GUIDES

Sandra Cisneros's
The House
on Mango Street

CURRENTLY AVAILABLE

1984
All the Pretty Horses
Beloved
Brave New World
Cry, The Beloved Country
Death of a Salesman
Hamlet
The Handmaid's Tale
The House on Mango Street
I Know Why the Caged Bird Sings
The Scarlet Letter
To Kill a Mockingbird

Bloom's
GUIDES

Sandra Cisneros's
The House
on Mango Street

Edited & with an Introduction
by Harold Bloom

CHELSEA HOUSE
PUBLISHERS
A Haights Cross Communications ◆ Company
Philadelphia

© 2004 by Chelsea House Publishers, a subsidiary of Haights Cross Communications.

A Haights Cross Communications Company

Introduction © 2004 by Harold Bloom.

Printed and bound in the United States of America.

First Printing
1 3 5 7 9 8 6 4 2

ISBN: 0-7910-7565-6

Chelsea House Publishers
1974 Sproul Road, Suite 400
Broomall, PA 19008-0914

www.chelseahouse.com

Contributing editor: Camille-Yvette Welsch

Cover series and design by Takeshi Takahashi

Layout by EJB Publishing Services

Contents

Introduction

Rereading *The House on Mango Street*, some years after first encountering this book by Sandra Cisneros, is not for me a literary experience. What matters about this series of linked narratives is social testimony, or the anguish of a young woman confronting the dilemmas of Mexican-American identity. To an outsider, these in turn seem founded upon the vexed issue of Mexican national identity. As background (one among many) to *The House on Mango Street*, I suggest that we turn to the greatest of Mexican writers, the poet-critic and Nobel Prize Winner, Octavio Paz (1914–1998). His *The Labyrinth of Solitude* (1950) remains a disturbing guide to what could be called the Mexican myth of Mexico.

Doubtless there are and will be rival attempts to define what might be called the genius of Mexico, and some Mexican feminists already denounce *The Labyrinth of Solitude* for implicitly taking the side of what it exposes and criticizes, the Mexican male myth that their women first betrayed them to, and with, the invading Spaniards. And yet I cannot see how Paz could have been clearer:

> In contrast to Guadalupe, who is the Virgin Mother, the *Chingada* is the violated Mother. Neither in her nor in the Virgin do we find traces of the darker attributes of the great goddesses: the lasciviousness of Amaterasu and Aphrodite, the cruelty of Artemis and Astarte, the sinister magic of Circe or the bloodlust of Kali. Both of them are passive figures. Guadalupe is pure receptivity, and the benefits she bestows are of the same order: she consoles, quiets, dries tears, calms passions. The *Chingada* is even more passive. Her passivity is abject: she does not resist violence, but is an inert heap of bones, blood and dust. Her taint is constitutional and resides, as we have said

7

earlier, in her sex. This passivity, open to the outside world, causes her to lose her identity: she is the *Chingada*. She loses her name; she is no one; she disappears into nothingness; she is Nothingness. And yet she is the cruel incarnation of the feminine condition.

If the *Chingada* is a representation of the violated Mother, it is appropriate to associate her with the Conquest, which was also a violation, not only in the historical sense but also in the very flesh of Indian women. The symbol of this violation is Doña Malinche, the mistress of Cortés. It is true that she gave herself voluntarily to the conquistador, but he forgot her as soon as her usefulness was over. Doña Marina [the name given to La Malinche by the Spaniards] becomes a figure representing the Indian women who were fascinated, violated or seduced by the Spaniards. As a small boy will not forgive his mother if she abandons him to search for his father, the Mexican people have not forgiven La Malinche for her betrayal. She embodies the open, the *chingado*, to our closed, stoic, impassive Indians. Cuauhtémoc and Doña Marina are thus two antagonistic and complementary figures. There is nothing surprising about our cult of the young emperor—"the only hero at the summit of art," an image of the sacrificed son—and there is also nothing surprising about the curse that weighs against La Malinche. This explains the success of the contemptuous adjective *malinchista* recently put into circulation by the newspapers to denounce all those who have been corrupted by foreign influences. The *malinchistas* are those who want Mexico to open itself to the outside world: the true sons of Malinche, who is the *Chingada* in person. Once again we see the opposition of the close and the open.

The Mexicans thus see themselves as the sons of La Malinche, and regard her as the *Chingada* personified. Since Paz was writing as a poet, he received all the misunderstandings that he risked: "an elegant insult against Mexican mothers." More accurately, as Paz remarked, "*The Labyrinth of Solitude* was an attempt to describe and understand certain myths; at the same time, insofar as it is a literary work, it has in turn become another myth."

In his *Distant Neighbors: A Portrait of the Mexicans* (1985), Alan Riding tends to agree with Paz:

The Mexican male's insecurity is best illustrated by his constant fear of betrayal by women. A contemporary anthropological explanation remains appealingly neat: Mexico's *mestizaje* began with the mating of Spanish men and Indian women, thus immediately injecting into the male-female relationship the concepts of betrayal by women and conquest, domination, force, and even rape by men. Just as the conqueror could never fully trust the conquered, today's *macho* must therefore brace himself against betrayal. Combining the Spaniard's obsession with honor and the Indian's humiliation at seeing his woman taken by force, Mexico's peculiarly perverse form of *machismo* thus emerges: the Spaniard's defense of honor becomes the Mexican's defense of his fragile masculinity.

In practice, this takes the form of worship of the female ideal, exemplified by the image of the long-suffering, abnegated and "pure" Virgin of Guadalupe and personified by each Mexican's own mother, who is seen as the giver of life and therefore incapable of betrayal. Conversely, the wife, who as an object of sex is considered an aberration from feminine perfection, must be humiliated, since a husband's faithfulness or excessive affection would imply vulnerability and weakness. Mistresses provide the man the opportunity to conquer and to betray in anticipation of betrayal. The wife's resentment toward her husband is then translated into smothering love for her son, who in turn elevates her to the status of female ideal but adopts his father's example as a husband.

Whether or not Cisneros agrees with Paz and Riding, I cannot know, but their melancholy observations help me to contexualize *The House on Mango Street*.

Biographical Sketch

Sandra Cisneros was born on December 20, 1954 to a Chicana mother and Mexican father in the suburbs of Chicago, Illinois. Her family, which included six brothers, moved frequently between Mexico City and Chicago. With her transient lifestyle and Chicana minority status, it was difficult for Cisneros to make and keep friends; consequently she became introverted and shy. At a young age Cisneros began observing people—taking notes on their actions and conversations in a spiral notebook which she carried with her, and later incorporating her observations into the poetry and short stories she wrote when she was in grade school.

Cisneros read widely and wrote throughout her adolescence, though her inhibitions kept her from academic success as she was too shy to speak up in class. In the tenth grade, however, one of her teachers encouraged her to read some of her stories to the class. Cisneros received positive feedback from the class and gained confidence. She began working on the school's literary magazine and eventually became its editor. Henceforth, Cisneros became "the poet" to her classmates.

Cisneros continued her education at Loyola University in Chicago, and in 1976 she earned a BA in English. In the late 1970's, Cisneros's writing talent gained her admittance to the famed University of Iowa Writers' Workshop. The workshop proved to be a turning point for her as she found her writer's voice. It was during writing exercises in these workshops that she realized her own experiences were quite different than the rest of the students in the class as well as from the majority of Americans. From this point on, Cisneros decided to incorporate her experiences as an underprivileged bicultural Chicana female growing up in America into her writing. To this day, Cisneros relies heavily on her own memories when developing storylines for her strong, independent, female characters. Her "awakening" experience in the writers' workshop eventually led her to write *The House on Mango Street*, which was published by Arte Publico Press in 1984 and won the Before Columbus Foundation's American Book Award in 1985.

After obtaining her master's degree, Cisneros spent three years teaching at a Latino Youth Alternative High School in Chicago. In the 1980s Cisneros earned a variety of fellowships and guest lectureships including two from the National Endowment for the Arts, one for fiction (1982) and one for poetry (1987). During this time, Cisneros wrote a collection of poetry entitled *My Wicked, Wicked Ways* (1987). Susan Bergholz, her literary agent, encouraged her to publish a collection of short stories, which were completed and published as *Woman Hollering Creek* in 1991 to wide acclaim. The collection won the PEN Center West Award for Best Fiction of 1991, the *Quality* Paperback Book Club New Voices Award, the Anisfield-Wolf Book Award, the Lannan Foundation Literary Award, and was selected as a noteworthy book of the year by *The New York Times* and the *American Library Journal*. In 1995, Cisneros won the prestigious MacArthur Foundation Fellowship.

Sandra Cisneros's body of work includes three volumes of fiction, *Caramelo* (2002), *The House on Mango Street* (1983) and *Woman Hollering Creek and Other Stories* (1991), and four volumes of poetry, *Bad Boys* (1980), *The Rodrigo Poems* (1985), *My Wicked, Wicked Ways* (1987), and *Loose Woman* (1994). She is also the author of a bilingual children's book, *Hairs/Pelitos* (1994).

The Story Behind the Story

As a young girl growing up in multiple urban spaces, Sandra Cisneros endured many of the same growing pains as her protagonist, Esperanza, though the more she became removed from her upbringing the further she found herself from the material that would eventually make her famous. Government aid enabled her to attend college and while there, a writer-in-residence encouraged her to attend graduate school. On that recommendation, Cisneros applied and was accepted into the Iowa Writers' Workshop, the most prestigious graduate writing program in the country. In an interview with Martha Satz given in 1985, Cisneros said "It was a bit of a shock to be in a program like the one at Iowa. It's a disciplined and rigorous program. I think I entered there a different person from the one who left." During her first year in the program, Cisneros found she was so intimidated that she wrote nearly nothing. She was the only person of Latino descent, much less Chicana, and her background of urban, multi-ethnic living distanced her from the other students.

In a now infamous class, Cisneros and her fellow students were discussing Gaston Bachelard's *Poetics of Space* wherein her professor referred to the "house of memory" as a comforting conceptual space. Cisneros vociferously contested the notion, believing that this concept could only be thought comforting by a man who had neither cleaned nor cared for a house. She knew her point of view was different, that she viewed words like "home" and "memory" with an uneasiness that none of her fellow students felt. Home had long been a word for ramshackle houses that embarrassed her, and her memory was filled with a host of multi-ethnic characters from the streets of the barrio. In retrospect, Cisneros commented "I think it was important for me to have the culture shock I experienced at Iowa, for me to experience my otherness, in order for me to choose my subject intentionally." Ultimately it forced her to consider what she could write about that no one else could.

That *something* was the *barrio* and Cisneros began to write about her experiences.

After graduating with her MA from Iowa in 1978, Cisneros went to work at Latino Youth Alternative High School in Chicago. In many respects, the job returned her to her childhood roots. Though the students drained her emotionally, they also provided her with more stories to add to her own memories of coming of age in the city. After that, she worked at Loyola University of Chicago as an administrative assistant and counselor to minority and disadvantaged students. When she saw their hopeless situations, she vowed to "give back" in some way. Armed with her own stories and devoted to telling the stories of her mother, her aunt, herself, and the other Chicana women and disenfranchised people around her, Cisneros began writing *The House on Mango Street*.

She claims that *Mango* came from her desire to add perspective to the barrio stories told by men. In her interview with Martha Satz, she recalled:

> I have lived in the barrio, but I discovered later on in looking at works by my contemporaries that they write about the barrio as a colorful, Sesame Street-like, funky neighborhood. To me the barrio was a repressive community. I found it frightening and very terrifying for a woman. The future for women in the barrio is not a wonderful one. You don't wander around these "mean streets." You stay at home. If you do have to get somewhere, you take your life in your hands. So I wanted to counter those colorful viewpoints, which I'm sure are true to an extent but were not true for me.

Her fresh perspective intrigued both critics and readers.

When the book first appeared in print, critics were generally pleased with the authentic voice, the attention to detail, the music of the language and the sheer impact of the coming-of-age story. In fact, Cisneros was awarded the *Before Columbus American Book Award* in 1985. Still, some critics took exception to her portrayal of men, claiming that it was too generalized, portraying all men as predatory and dangerous. Others claimed that it was particularly insulting to Chicano men and destructive to their already compromised persona in the mass media. Still others objected to Cisneros's refusal to pin her book down to a specific genre, thereby forcing critics to re-evaluate the way in which they judge her writing. The book is part prose poetry, part novel, and part young girl's diary. Despite its critics, Cisneros and her book have enjoyed much success. *Mango* appears in collegiate course listings and elementary schools, book clubs, and senior citizens homes in spite of its multi-cultural feminist politics and child protagonist. Although *Mango* was originally published by a small press, Arte Publico, Random House eventually opted to acquire the publishing rights. The move, six years after its initial publication, from a small press to a world-wide publishing conglomerate, suggests that *The House on Mango Street* has earned its place among the best contemporary coming-of-age novels.

List of Characters

Esperanza Cordero is the adolescent protagonist who tells her coming-of-age story through vignettes relating what she sees and feels in addition to the actual events of her life. She dreams throughout the narrative for a house of her own which she eventually understands will be realized through writing.

Nenny is Esperanza's little sister. Throughout the novel, Esperanza feels more and more separated from her younger sister, due to her own maturation. Her sister is also the only person with whom Esperanza shares an intimate understanding of what it means to live in Mexico, thereby reinforcing her close ties to family.

Mama is a very accomplished and talented woman who chooses to leave school because she does not consider her clothes nice enough for public consumption. As a result of her regret, she urges Esperanza to embrace education and learn all she can so that she will not be dependent or feel trapped.

Papa is a gardener for the wealthy. Esperanza often defines him by what he allows and does not allow her to do.

Carlos and Kiki are Esperanza's brothers. They communicate with their sisters inside the house, but outside they ignore her, maintaining the gender strata of the neighborhood.

Cathy is a neighborhood girl who befriends Esperanza for a week before her family moves to a more expensive, less Latino neighborhood. Her brief presence in the story reinforces the transient nature of the barrio and the socioeconomic stratification between ethnic groups.

Lucy and Rachel are girls from Texas who befriend Esperanza, with whom she buys a part in a bike. With them, Esperanza comes of age, reinforcing the idea that for Chicanas the experience of acculturation is communal.

Meme Ortiz is a boy who moves into Cathy's old house and with whom Esperanza has a jumping contest. Meme's desire to prove himself in the new neighborhood overwhelms his common sense as he breaks both of his arms trying to win the contest. His broken arms suggest that few can escape the barrio.

Marin is Esperanza's cousin who lives in the basement apartment of the Ortiz's. She becomes an example of the Chicana female—beautiful but stuck in the house babysitting. Her sexual power is curtailed by the men of her family, and it is also the only means by which she might escape her current life. She must barter her body for marriage in order to escape the barrio. Through her, Esperanza gains awareness of the ways in which her gender can empower or imprison her.

Louie's cousin, though never given a specific name, is important because he returns to the neighborhood in a Cadillac convertible to show what he has accomplished. Sadly, the accomplishment is false but it strengthens Esperanza's resolve to return to her community with work of real merit. Louie's cousin is also an example of the way the children of the barrio view him as a friend rather than a criminal because of his relation to members of the community.

Rose Vargas is a woman with too many ill-behaved children. She is another victim of the patriarchal system in Chicano culture. Because Rose's husband has left her to care for so many children alone, everyone in the community, including Rose and her children, see her problem as being too big to remedy and thereby cease to care about the welfare of the Vargas children.

Alicia is an older girl in the neighborhood who attends college as a way to escape her life as surrogate mother and wife after the death of her mother. She provides a positive role model for Esperanza as she has found a way out of the barrio through education.

Darius is a bully who picks on girls and skips school. He does, however, say something profound that Esperanza will remember for the rest of her life. He points at the clouds and tells Esperanza, "That's God." Esperanza is moved by this simple expression of faith, found even in the barrio.

Aunt Lupe is Esperanza's aunt, a woman who was formerly a powerful swimmer. Sadly, Lupe, he has been stricken by an illness which eventually kills her. She urges Esperanza to never stop writing.

Elenita is the witch woman who tells fortunes and predicts that Esperanza will have a house of her own, "a home in the heart." Her prediction is important because Esperanza begins to think of home as something created on the interior, as a collection of stories and understanding.

Geraldo is the young man who is killed by a hit and run accident while Marin is with him. For Esperanza, Geraldo becomes a symbol of the way in which identity is lost between Mexico and the United States. He belongs to no country and no one claims him when he dies.

Ruthie lives with her mother, Edna, who owns the large building next door to Esperanza. She comes to live with her mother after her marriage fails. It is unclear whether marriage caused her child-like mental state or whether her mental state causes the dissolution of the marriage. Ruthie claims that she used to write children's books. Esperanza befriends her, showing her compassion and commitment to the disenfranchised.

Sire is a neighborhood boy who looks at Esperanza as a sexual being and in so doing arouses in her feelings of sexual awakening.

Mamacita is the large, beautiful, Mexican woman who moves into the neighborhood. She is bereft at having to leave her country and Esperanza empathizes with her feelings of dislocation and her powerlessness in controlling what happens to her.

Rafaela is a young woman married to a man who keeps her locked in the house. She leans out her window and dreams of another life, and becomes for Esperanza an example of how men imprison women to control and suppress their sexual power.

Sally is a young woman about Esperanza's age whose father beats her and imprisons her in his home out of fear of her sexual power.

Minerva is a young woman only a little older than the adolescent Esperanza, who has two children and a husband who beats her. Minerva and Esperanza share their poetry with each other. She serves as a cautionary tale to Esperanza, reinforcing the idea that sometimes marriage is not an escape but a potential prison in and of itself.

The Three Sisters are elderly aunts of Lucy and Rachel. They tell Esperanza that she will escape from the barrio but that she must return for the others who cannot leave.

Summary and Analysis

Before entering the text, readers receive insight into Cisneros's project with her dedication, "A las Mujeres to the Women." She dedicates her book in both English and Spanish, reinforcing her own dual ethnic background, to the women of her life. In doing so, she also acknowledges that a large part of her struggle for identity in the barrio was driven by issues of gender.

Cisneros chooses to tell the story in a series of vignettes which claim their own liminal space. The stories resist assignation to a particular form, floating comfortably between prose poetry, the novel, and journal writing. In many ways, resistance is the core of the book. Cisneros's *The House on Mango Street* resists form, gender stereotypes, cultural norms, and pre-fabricated futures for the characters involved.

Cisneros chooses to use the voice of a child in the throes of puberty to tell her story. This is a savvy choice, allowing Esperanza to observe without passing judgment. Readers, therefore, bring their own cultural associations to the significant details Esperanza presents. Cisneros keeps her authorial intrusion minimal with the girl's voice, thereby resisting the urge to be overtly political.

The book opens with a chapter of the same name, setting the scene early and offering information that contextualizes the house and its significance to the family. Esperanza, the title character, a girl on the brink of puberty explains "We didn't always live on Mango Street." What she remembers from her early childhood is moving from one place to another as the family grew larger and needed more space. Eventually, they find the house on Mango Street, and although the children have more freedom here to make noise and play without the interference of other children from the apartment building, it still does not fulfill Esperanza's (or her family's) expectations for a first house. Her parents have little choice in what they buy due to a meager budget and a compelling impetus to move. The house on Mango Street represents the best of the Cordero family's options, but for Esperanza, whose dreams were based on the houses she saw on television, her small ramshackle house with its one bedroom for an entire family of six is shameful and depressing. Critic Julian Olivarez claims "Mango Street is a street sign, a marker, that circumscribes the neighborhood to its Latino population of Puerto Ricans, Chicanos, and Mexican immigrants. This house is not the protagonist's dream house; it is only a temporary house" (235). Esperanza recalls feeling ashamed from an incident in the past when a nun asked her to point her home out in their former neighberhood on Loomis Street. The nun's disgusted and incredulous tone when Esperanza points the dilapidated third floor of a house shames the child. The nun's assumption is clearly based on ethnic stereotypes, and though Esperanza doesn't acknowledge this, the woman's comments and incredulity make Esperanza "feel like nothing." The first chapter ends with Esperanza's fervent statement of her quest. "I knew then that I had to have a house. A real house. One I could point to." The "sad red house" is not the sort of home to be proud of, not like the ones on TV, and though her parents keep saying that the house is a temporary solution, she doesn't believe them. Esperanza realizes that her family will never be able to provide more than the temporary houses in which they have been living. This reinforces her desire and drive to eventually own a respectable home of her own.

Within this first chapter, Esperanza immediately indicates the gap between the white middle class families portrayed on TV and the Latino experience in the barrio of Chicago. The white world has three bathrooms to the Cordero's one, and enough bedrooms for every child to have his or her own. Esperanza also recognizes that in order to participate in the broader white American world she needs to have an expression of belonging through her house, a visible manifestation of success and assimilation. For her, the home is a way to assume a public persona and eventually a place wherein she might assume an identity for her community. Her identity becomes inextricably interconnected with her home environment. Leslie Guiterrez-Jones articulates Esperanza's desire:

Acutely aware of the disempowerment that results from lacking "a home of one's own," she yearns to stake out an architectural space—one which she implicitly assumes will provide her with the "space" to develop a sense of identity and an artistic voice. However, when architecture will not cooperate, she must look instead to her imagination in order to create a sense of space—one which can, in turn, provide a place for her writing. (296)

In the next chapter, **"Hair,"** Esperanza provides us with a strong sense of her domesticated mother. The girl associates the smell of bread with her mother's hair. She speaks of the pin curls her mother makes in an effort to look pretty and the way her mother moves over to make room in the bed for her children while her Papa sleeps blissfully through the commotion. Esperanza remembers the sounds of rain and her father's snoring as her mother holds her. Within this description, the mother belongs exclusively to the family and the household she runs. It is Mama who makes room in the bed when a child is scared and Papa who remains asleep and unaware of the goings on around him. Throughout the vignette, Esperanza's depictions recreate a sense of comfort and belonging, subtly reinforcing the strength of her family ties.

In the chapter entitled, **"Boys & Girls,"** Esperanza continues her observations regarding gender and family. She points out that in the Cordero home her siblings all speak with each other, but outside of it, the boys have their own lives and never interact with the girls. This segregation mimics the lives of the older people in the community and reinforces the gender stratifications outside of marriage. Without her brothers, Esperanza is left with her younger sister, Nenny. Nenny is too young to be the friend that Esperanza wants, one to whom she will not have to explain jokes, one to whom she can tell her secrets. The short chapter ends with Esperanza dreaming of being a red balloon, "a balloon tied to an anchor." Clearly, the balloon is a metaphor for escape, one of many throughout the book, but equally clear is the pull of her familial duties. An anchor tied to the balloon keeps it earthbound and stationary, which represents Nenny's association to Esperanza in the story.

Esperanza's observations of cultural disparity continue as she critically examines her name in **"My Name."** In America, it means hope; in Spanish, it means sorrow. To Esperanza, it means bad luck and ill fate, and the sounds of her father's Mexican records. She associates grief and bad luck with her Spanish name due to her namesake, her great-grandmother, who like her descendant was born "in the Chinese year of the horse—which is supposed to be bad luck if you're born female." Esperanza doesn't believe this, insisting it is yet another story meant to keep women oppressed and powerless. She says, "I think this is a Chinese lie, because the Chinese, like the Mexicans, don't like their woman strong." This observation pinpoints Esperanza's awareness of what kind of life the women lead within her community. She resists the idea of women being powerless, preferring instead the legends of her wild grandmother who refused to marry. Esperanza explains further how her willful grandmother was abducted and forced to marry. She tells us how her grandmother was carried off "as if she were a fancy chandelier."

This story teaches Esperanza that to be a woman is to be a commodity, one that can be bought, sold and even stolen. She continues the story, claiming that her grandmother never forgave her grandfather, instead she spent the rest of her life looking out a window, "the way so many women sit their sadness on an elbow." This image of women staring out windows pining for some sort of freedom or independence from their husbands or fathers is one that returns throughout the book. For Esperanza, it figures as a prison with a princess hidden away never to come out. In her world, princes do not rescue but imprison the princess. As she continues to think on her name, she begins to wish for a name more like a superhero or a mythic woman, giving in to her dream of escape. Critic Tomoko Kuribayashi claims that "Cisneros' narrative highlights how language—and taking control of it—is a determining factor for Esperanza's future. Taking control of language is taking control of one's spatial experiences" (169). In a way, it means writing oneself out of one's current destiny. Critic Julian Olivarez sees Esperanza's renaming as a way of denying the patriarchy: "Esperanza prefers a name not culturally embedded in a dominating, male-centered ideology" (236).

"Cathy, Queen of Cats" is both the title of the next chapter and the girl who offers Esperanza advice on who to associate with in their area, basing her suggestions on societal prejudices. Cathy tells her to stay away from a man whom she calls "the baby-grabber," two "raggedy" girls, and a woman who became stuck up after college. There is also a woman who used to own an apartment building and begged her son not to sell it. The son agreed but then sold the building anyway. Cathy figures men as evil, selling things out from under women, preying on innocents, reinforcing Esperanza's idea that men are dangerous and oppressive. After observing Esperanza, Cathy agrees to be her friend, but only for a week. Her family is moving to a better neighborhood, because she says "the neighborhood is getting bad." Even though Esperanza is young, she is wise enough to realize two things about Cathy and her family. One, Cathy is simply repeating what she hears her parents say and two, Cathy's parents are moving because of the neighborhood influx of Chicano families like her own.

Esperanza does eventually have a good day in her new neighborhood. While walking with Cathy, her temporary friend, Esperanza meets Rachel and Lucy, rag tag sisters from Texas, who want five dollars for their friendship so they can buy a new bike. Esperanza, desperate for friends and some sign that she fits in, takes three of her own dollars and two of her unknowing sister's and invests in the bike, losing snobbish Cathy in the process but acquiring two non-judgmental friends and a mode of escape, the bike. The three girls agree to take turns, each owning the bike once every three days. The ownership of the bike speaks to the circumstances of the barrio. To own something requires the aid of others as few people can afford to buy things on their own. It also speaks to the communal attitude which marks Esperanza's later comments regarding her house and her faith in writing. She intends to help others get out of their situations.

In the next chapter, Esperanza turns her attention to her sister, Nenny, remarking that they look nothing alike at first glance, not like her new friends Lucy and Rachel whose facial features clearly indicate their relationship. Instead, the bond between Nenny and Esperanza shows in their mannerisms and in their shared cultural caché, acquired from years of living the same experience. When Esperanza comments "Look at that house ... it looks like Mexico," she is comforted by the fact that her sister understands. Nenny is one of the few people with whom Esperanza shares the same cultural literacy. This literacy, in some ways, exiles Esperanza from the people around her, but at the same time it strengthens her familial ties.

In **"Gil's Furniture Bought & Sold"** Esperanza ventures into the local junk store where everything is piled precariously and close. The store is a maze in which a child might get lost. At the center of Gil's is the old man who owns the shop. During one visit with her sister, Nenny finds an old music box and asks the owner about it. He winds the victrola and sounds pours out, entrancing both Esperanza and Nenny. A moment later, Esperanza catches herself being interested, so she turns away, pretending that she doesn't care. She thinks her sister is stupid for caring and asking how much it costs. In this "are you tough enough" neighborhood, to show too much love for beauty is childish and dangerous, an admission of immaturity and weakness in and of itself.

In the next vignette, Esperanza describes her new neighbor, a young man who calls himself "Meme" though his name is Juan. He lives in Cathy, Queen of Cat's old house, a house built by Cathy's father with slanted floors and crooked stairs. It is in Meme's backyard that he and the neighborhood kids host the "First Annual Tarzan Jumping Contest." Meme wins but in the process breaks both of his arms. Winning is important to the children and Meme willingly accepts the consequences. He has proven himself in the neighborhood and feels good about it.

Downstairs from the Ortiz's, in the rented basement apartment, live Louie's family, from Puerto Rico. His cousin

Marin lives with them, and though she wears make-up and nylons and claims to be in love, her nearest contact with the outside world is in the doorway of her home. She is forced into babysitting her siblings because she is a woman, an early example of the imprisoned women that Esperanza observes throughout the book. Louie's other cousin drives into the neighborhood one afternoon in a yellow Cadillac convertible. All of the children clamor for rides, asking the man where he got the car. He never answers them but he does take them for a ride around the neighborhood. Intoxicated with the power windows and luxury of the Cadillac, the children press buttons and play with controls. By the seventh time around the block, police sirens are sounding. Louie's cousin orders all of the children out of the car and speeds off. The chase ends with the car crashing into a tree and the young man in handcuffs. His return to the neighborhood speaks to Esperanza's dream of leaving the barrio and returning for the others a success story. This young man comes back to his neighborhood to prove what he has achieved (however nefarious). Sadly, he also gives the impression that one of the few ways out of the barrio is crime.

Marin becomes the focal point of the next chapter, **"Marin."** Unlike Esperanza and her friends, Marin wears make-up and understands boys. She dreams of working downtown in a job where she can wear nice clothes and be seen by men, with the hope that one might marry her and take her away to his home in the suburbs. Every night she stands on the front porch after her mother goes to sleep and waits for the boys to come around and look at her. Esperanza, in her careful study of Marin as a female archetype realizes that Marin has pinned all of her hopes of escape on men. Marriage is Marin's chosen escape from the barrio. Olivarez sees this as a continuation of the "dialect of inside/outside, of confinement and desire for the freedom of the outside world ..." (234).

Esperanza directly addresses race and ethnicity and their relation to inclusion and exclusion in **"Those Who Don't."** She watches people come into her neighborhood, scared that they will be attacked. Here, "All brown all around" there is no difference to fear. She knows every strange figure in the neighborhood. Even when Louie's cousin returns in an early chapter with his stolen car, the children greet him as a friend, because of his relation to the neighborhood. With knowledge comes lack of fear and with that, a kind of power. Still, she recognizes that white people are not the sole perpetuators of racial distrust. She notes that her family also rolls the windows up tight in a neighborhood "of another color." She muses that this is "how it goes and goes."

In the next chapter, Esperanza introduces Rose Vargas and her multitude of ill-behaved children. Because there are so many and they behave so badly, the entire community including the children and Rose, become indifferent to the well-being of these children. As a result, no one notices when Angel Vargas, a small child, climbs to the top of roof and throws herself off. Esperanza outlines the apathy created when people are overwhelmed.

In **"Alicia Who Sees Mice,"** Esperanza again comments on the fate of women in her culture. Alicia is a young woman in the neighborhood who attends college, believing that education might get her out of the neighborhood. She is also a surrogate mother to her siblings and a surrogate housekeeper for her father. She has inherited her "mama's rolling pin and sleepiness," and wakes early to make tortillas. Olivarez notes, that "Here we do not see the tortilla as a symbol of cultural identity but as a symbol of a subjugating ideology, of sexual domination, of the imposition of a role that the young woman must assume" (237). This young woman goes to bed so exhausted she hallucinates mice who keep her up at night. Her father orders her to sleep so she can again wake early and provide for her siblings before taking two trains and a bus to college, which might prove to be her salvation from marriage or life in a factory.

In the next chapter, Esperanza introduces Darius who bullies little girls and skips school. Esperanza talks about the sky being one of the few beautiful things that exist in the barrio. This thought reminds her of Darius and a profound thing her once said to her. He had been looking at the sky and then pointed to the clouds telling her, "That's God." Esperanza marvels at how simple and true that is. The sky is one of the beautiful things that make it into the barrio, and it cannot be taken away based on money or prejudice.

The topic of clouds comes up again in **"And Some More."** Esperanza, Nenny, Rachel, and Lucy begin to talk about the number of different Eskimo names for snow. In the next lines, they bicker about the type of snow and the number of names a cousin has, at least one for each identity (American and Spanish) and they come to rest on the different names of clouds. As they identify the different types of clouds, names from the neighborhood are being repeated, all the different types of people who live in the barrio, all the different types of Spanish names. The girls break into argument over a description of a cloud that includes a reference to a face. They try to out-talk each other, exchanging insults and eventually creating a cacophony of voices. The chapter ends with the girls realizing that their argument is stupid and not worth risking their friendship over. Critic Leslie Gutierrez-Jones believes that the competing voices symbolize Cisneros's emphasis on communal and collective identity making. Guiterrez-Jones writes:

> The competing voices eventually blend to produce a sort of harmony—even a wry simple wisdom—in a way that monologic narrative would not allow. Such rhetorical instances mark yet another aspect of Esperanza's unique development toward an artistic voice and a sense of self which achieves an ongoing balance between connection and separation (309).

In **"The Family of Little Feet,"** the girls have another collective experience when they receive a bag of shoes from a family in the neighborhood. The multi-colored shoes are exciting to the girls, offering them the chance to pretend to be Cinderella, or an older girl who attracts men like flies. As they swap shoes and try them on, Lucy orders them to take their socks off, and when they do they realize that they have legs like the older girls, the kind that signal to men. They walk down the street to the grocery store. Around them, the men are abuzz, some indignant and wanting to protect the girls from growing up too quickly, some with lascivious intent. The grocer tells the girls to take the high heels off claiming "Them are dangerous," and a boy on a bicycle cries out "Ladies, lead me to heaven." So unaccustomed are they to being viewed as adults it takes the girls a few moments to realize that he is speaking to them. Critic Michelle Scalise Sugiyama writes:

> Their resolution to never go back to wearing the other kind' of shoes comes after they realize that the shoes make them sexually attractive to men ... This power to arouse men and to make women jealous initially exhilarates them—they 'just keep strutting", enjoying for the moment their position as the source of power rather than the object (10).

As they pass the laundromat, they even make other women jealous with the shoes they have. Their sense of empowerment dies, however, when they meet a bum who compliments them and offers a dollar for a kiss. Suddenly, the male attention that brought so much pleasure is now rife with potential violence. The girls run from him and decide they are tired of being beautiful. For the first time, they encounter the hungry gaze of the male sexual predator and the experience so frightens them that when Lucy's mother throws the shoes out a few days later, none of the girls utters a whisper of complaint.

"A Rice Sandwich" chronicles another epiphany for Esperanza. Everyday she goes home for lunch, envying the children who remain at school to eat in the cafeteria. The cafeteria or "canteen" as she calls it, becomes a fixation for Esperanza; she desires to know what goes on in that room and convinces her mother to write a note to school explaining that Esperanza is too weak to walk to and from school in the middle of the day. The sister allows her to stay at school for one day and Esperanza gets her wish; she goes to the canteen but only after meeting with Mother Superior who questions her until

Esperanza is in tears. In her office, the nun unwilling to grant the girl's request, asks Esperanza to point her house out, saying, "'You don't live far, she says ... I bet I can see your house from my window. Which one?' she said pointing to a row of ugly 3-flats, the ones even the raggedy men are ashamed to go to. Yes, I nodded even though I knew that wasn't my house and began to cry." The experience reveals for Esperanza the nun's beliefs concerning the possibilities for Mexican families. Critic Ellen McCracken believes that this strengthens Esperanza's resolve:

> It is in response to humiliations such as these that the autobiographical protagonist expresses a need for a house of her own. Rather than mere desire to possess private property, Esperanza's wish for a house represents a positive objectification of the self, the chance to redress humiliation and establish a dignified sense of her own personhood (65).

When she finally enters the canteen, she is crying, her lunch is soggy, and all of the other children are watching her. After all of her persuasive rhetoric, Esperanza finds she no longer wants to be in this hostile environment that turns out to be nothing very interesting at all. Again, she is forced to recognize the boundaries of inclusion and exclusion.

In **"Chanclas"** Esperanza shops with her mother for a new dress to wear to her cousin's baptism. Her mother buys her a new dress, slip, and socks. By the end of the trip, her mother is too tired to buy Esperanza new shoes and they leave without them. While her mother is shopping, Esperanza waits by the door, allowing no one in except her mother, another small reality of her life. She dresses for the party and puts on her old shoes, feeling sure that they have overshadowed the effect of the rest of her pretty things. Again, Esperanza returns to the eroticism of the feet. When she arrives at the party, she sits in a chair, tucking her feet beneath the seat in an effort to hide them. When she is asked to dance by a boy, she refuses, afraid to show her shoes. Her Uncle Nacho then asks her to dance and drags the unwilling Esperanza to the floor. Her body follows her uncle's lead, remembering all that it was taught about dancing and the two are complimented by the people watching. With all of the compliments and fanfare, Esperanza eventually forgets that her shoes are old and serviceable, bought because they last. Instead, all she hears is the clapping of the crowd as the music stops. When she returns to her seat, her mother is proud. Throughout the rest of the night, the boy who asked her to dance, who she suddenly sees as a man, watches her. She is excited by the idea of being wanted by this man. Scalise Sugiyama notes that:

> Esperanza's self-esteem is dependent upon the arousing male interest ... The male definition of beauty, exemplified by high heels, is psychologically as well as physically crippling as it requires, ultimately, submission and dependence. Compliance with this beauty standard is one of the ways in which, as Maria Herrara-Sobek puts it, 'women are socialized into being participants in their own oppression' (18).

Esperanza is becoming increasingly aware of her sexuality and the powers and limits that accompany it. This becomes particularly apparent in the next chapter.

"Hips" is a particularly pivotal chapter because Esperanza emphatically articulates the chasm caused by age and knowledge between herself and her sister, Nenny. The chapter begins with Lucy, Rachel, Esperanza and Nenny skipping rope, talking about hips. Rachel claims "They're good for holding a baby while you're cooking." Esperanza immediately feels disgusted. Rachel cannot move outside of her own knowledge to imagine something different, beyond gender roles. Lucy suggests hips are needed to dance. Nenny claims that without them, one becomes a boy. Esperanza counters all arguments with science, an Anglo, seemingly infallible discipline, a source she derived from the college-girl, Alicia. Hips widen to allow mothers to give birth to their children. Beyond science though, Esperanza wants to discuss a broader, more imminent question. Do they want them? Will they know what to do with them once they get them? The questions reflect her insecurities about taking on both the body and the roles of a woman, and the possible co-modification of both. Esperanza describes a woman's walk saying "like if half of you wanted to go one way and the other half the other" (50). Nenny answers naively that the walk is meant to rock babies and Esperanza immediately wants to discount her younger sibling, but after thinking she realizes that this idea may not be so far-fetched and that her sister may not be so distant from her after all. Lucy starts to dance, claiming that "you gotta get the rhythm," and the girls begin to concoct rhymes that match the rhythm of the dances. While the older girls are chanting their new rhymes, Nenny continues to chant the old ones she already knows. Esperanza's fierce protection of her sister keeps the other girls from saying anything, but it doesn't keep Esperanza from thinking once again that her sister is still a child and that she, Esperanza, and their friends, Lucy and Rachel, have transcended that stage of their life. As Olivarez puts it:

> Suddenly the awareness of time passing and of growing up is given a spatial dimension. Esperanza, on the outside, is looking at Nenny inside the arc of the swinging rope that now separates Nenny's childhood dimension from her present awareness of just having left behind that very same childhood (238).

The girls, excluding Nenny, are now well on their way into puberty and with that comes the acquisition of a certain set of culturally derived expectations based on gender and socioeconomic status.

One such expectation shown in the next story **"The First Job,"** is that the children in the family will get jobs to help their parents pay for the Catholic school they attend. For the Cordero family, there is no question of going to public school. Her father forbids it because "nobody goes to public school unless you wanted to turn out bad." His judgment is two-fold. First, he believes that a Catholic education will lead to spiritual success, particularly in light of the fact that it reinforces gender roles in the family, but also because inner city schools are notoriously poorly financed and maintained. In an effort to get a job quickly, Esperanza has already gotten her social security number and imagines herself working at a typical job in a dime store or a hot dog stand. When Esperanza comes home from school one day, her mother and her aunt are waiting for her with a job plan. She is to work at the Peter Pan Photo Finishers where her aunt works. They coach Esperanza to claim she is a year older than she actually is in order to begin working without the interference of child labor laws and her aunt leaves. The next morning, Esperanza puts on a navy dress that makes her look older than her years and borrows money for lunch and her fare, knowing that she has a full week before she gets paid from her new job. For the interview, she lies about her age and gets the job. At work, she wears gloves and matches photos with their negatives. The hours are long and she gets tired but is too shy to ask if she can sit. She mimics the behavior of the women beside her, gratefully sitting when they do. Her shyness backfires when the two women figure out what she is doing and laugh at her, telling her finally that she can sit down whenever she wants to. To hide her embarrassment, she relies on bravado, claiming that she already knew that, but their laughter only exacerbates her feelings of exclusion.

Her shyness continues to make the job difficult. When she is too scared to go into a lunchroom of strangers and eat, so she hides in the washroom, eating her lunch and resuming her work early. When the next break comes, she hides in the cloak room, watching people punch in for the next shift. While she sits there, an older Asian man sits down to talk to her. Esperanza is happy to have the company until the man claims it's his birthday and asks for a kiss. She figures that there is no harm in kissing an old man for his birthday, but when she moves to kiss his cheek, he grabs her face and forces a kiss onto her mouth. The older she becomes, the more Esperanza develops a need, born of experience, to view men as dangerous predators. This continued pattern of abuse, harassment and potential abuse upsets some critics as they say it is an unfair portrayal of men and Chicano men in particular.

Still, in contrast to that point of view, in the next chapter, Esperanza is awoken by her father. He tells her, in his native Spanish, that her grandmother is dead and then he begins to cry. This unsettles Esperanza. She associates few things with her father: his getting up for work in the dark, his thick hands and shoes, the water he combs his hair with and the coffee he drinks. His masculinity, his whole being for her, is encased in the daily rituals that surround his working and the effects of his work. To see her father cry is to see him as a human being as opposed to a breadwinner and an authority figure. She puts her arms around her father and holds him tight, wanting to never let go of this rare moment in which she gets to comfort him. She also recognizes that her father will have to return to Mexico for the funeral. This realization reinforces the notion that she is between two ethnicities, Mexican and American, and in many ways of neither as she negotiates her coming of age. As the eldest child in her family, and because her culture demands this order, it is her job to tell her siblings of their Grandmother's death and to keep them quiet out of respect for her father. Guiterrez-Jones links this moment to the idea that "The continuity between generations will remain unbroken; as her father weeps for the loss of his parent, Esperanza recognizes that some day she will in turn grieve his death—and will herself need to be held and held and held" (303–304). Suddenly, she is forced to face a very tangible mortality.

The notion of respect carries into the next vignette, **"Born Bad,"** as Esperanza relates the most evil deed she has ever committed. The chapter begins with her mother praying for Esperanza because she was born on an evil day. Her friends Lucy and Rachel pray too, for forgiveness for what they and Esperanza did to Aunt Lupe. Aunt Lupe is Esperanza's aunt, a woman formerly beautiful and vibrant, who has been laid low by disease. Esperanza's only knowledge of her aunt outside of her sick bed is from photos. In the photos her aunt is athletic, a swimmer. Though she tries, Esperanza cannot reconcile the photographs with the reality of her aunt who seems surrounded by a yellow scent, lighting, and bed clothes, as if the illness has infected everything in the room and turned it that sickly hue.

Aunt Lupe's illness makes Esperanza consider the nature of good and bad, and question who it is who deserves to go bad, searching for some karmic logic. She lists events she knows through pictures, trying to imagine the exact instant the illness bloomed in her aunt's body. She includes in her litany of guesses the suggestion that God was busy too, or what is perhaps the story told by her cousin, that her aunt fell very hard from a high stool. Ultimately, she accepts none of these stories, coming to the difficult assessment that disease is democratic and random. She muses too that sometimes because the disease is so omnipresent, one forgets that things were ever any other way, and that this woman is in very grave pain and so close to death.

During one visit to Aunt Lupe, the girls decide to include the ailing woman in a game they play. In the game, they select a famous person to imitate until someone guesses the identity correctly. During this particular game the girls decide that it would be fun to choose people from around the neighborhood to imitate rather than stars. They decide to imitate Aunt Lupe. Esperanza experiences conflicting feelings because she loves her aunt. Lupe is the only person who listens to every word she says. Esperanza would bring library books and read them to her. In one instance, she tried to show her aunt a picture, holding the book to the woman's face until she tells her niece that she is blind. Esperanza is ashamed but she returns to the woman's bedside often to share books and even her own poetry. When she finishes reading, her aunt compliments her, and though she is tired, she gives Esperanza the advice that she clings to all her life: "You just remember to keep writing, Esperanza. You must keep writing. It will keep you free." Though Esperanza promises her aunt she will follow the orders, she has no real idea, in that moment, what this will mean for her. Critic Tomoko Kuribayashi suggests that the event is part of a literary heritage: "Her disabled aunt, Lupe, listening to Esperanza's poems, encourages her to keep on writing, her advice embodying the strength Esperanza's culture and older women around her can give her" (172).

Aunt Lupe becomes an iconic figure for Esperanza. Lupe is one of the few women who encourage her to be self-reliant and independent, which makes Esperanza's guilt nearly overwhelming when she and her friends decide to do impressions of her. The girls make themselves limp and cry out for help in weak voices, they pretend to be blind and to have trouble sitting up. What they don't realize is that as they are enjoying their game, Aunt Lupe has died. They are shocked; they had nearly forgotten that the actions they imitated were those of a dying woman. The girls retreat into Catholicism to beg for forgiveness for their actions. Guitterez-Jones marks the moment as important in terms of collective experience:

> [t]he girls take on responsibility for her death, and Esperanza unsparingly shoulders her share of the burden for their communal guilt ... Such painful encounters with "difference" elucidate Esperanza's encounters with racial prejudice: with misunderstanding and fear born of ignorance, and with the phenomenon of not belonging . (305)

In the next chapter, **"Elenita, Cards, Palm, Water,"** Esperanza goes to the home of the local "witch woman" to have her palm read. Much of the expected mysticism of a fortune teller is missing in this home as Elenita is still a woman with a messy house, needy children, and plastic-covered furniture. Here, the mystical and the diurnal co-exist, as both Catholicism and older superstitions co-exist. When Esperanza enters Elenita's home, the fortune teller immediately tells her that today is a better day than yesterday, when the planets were off. Uncertainly, Esperanza agrees, and although she is listening to the television in the other room and wants to go watch cartoons like the baby, she chooses not to retreat into the childish endeavor. Her mission is to discover her future, and whether or not it contains a house. They stay in the kitchen where Elenita works between a collection of Catholic paraphernalia and a deck of tarot cards. She tells Esperanza to get the water. On the counter, there are a number of dirty glasses. Esperanza picks the only clean glass which has a beer logo on it. Even when practicing an ancient tradition, the Mexican and the American world converge, though the truth is in the bubbles, the bubbles are in the American glass.

Elenita asks Esperanza to look into the glass and tell her what she sees. Esperanza sees nothing. Elenita shrugs it off and makes the sign of the cross over the water three times and cuts the tarot cards. As Elenita works, Esperanza again finds herself distracted by the cartoons on the TV. She wants badly to go and watch them but she stays in the kitchen because, she thinks her whole life is "on that kitchen table: past, present, future." Elenita takes Esperanza's hand, looks into it, and closes her eyes. She begins to tell Esperanza what she sees. The most important revelations are the last two: "an anchor of arms" and "a home in the heart." With the anchor, she predicts community to be a part of Esperanza's identity as an adult. With the home in the heart, she predicts that Esperanza's desire to have a house of which she can be proud will manifest itself on the interior before she can have the structure. Her house is built by the stories and experiences of those around her, and by her own compassion and belief in bearing witness to those around her.

The predictions disappoint Esperanza with their vagueness, particularly in light of the very specific magic she knows Elenita is capable of dispensing for other problems like headaches and romantic conundrums. Elenita sees her disappointment and offers to read again, but Esperanza thanks her and gives her five dollars for the job. As they part, Esperanza is pondering the meaning of the prediction and Elenita is calling out a good-bye that consists of both the astrological and the sacred, emphasizing again the duality of beliefs in the barrio.

Esperanza is reminded again of Mexico in the next chapter when she tells the story of **"Geraldo No Last Name."** Marin, Esperanza's older neighbor who enchants the boys but is not allowed to leave the yard without permission, goes to dozens of dances in places that Esperanza lists like a litany of forbidden fantasy worlds. The chapter begins with Marin describing an encounter with a man: she met him at a dance, he was young, attractive, and worked in a restaurant. He wore "[G]reen pants and (a) Saturday shirt." Marin continues to explain what happened feeling defensive and self-conscious, asking "And how was she to know that she'd be the last one to see him alive." As she tells the story of the hit and run accident that killed him, she makes a point to repeat that she only met him that night, dancing. There is nothing more to connect them except their love of dancing. That's what she told the hospital and what she told the police. For all intents and purposes, Geraldo did not exist. He was without identification, without people in this country. Marin sat in the emergency room waiting for this man she didn't know, though she can't explain why as he was not a boyfriend or even anyone she had met before. Instead, she reduces him to just another new immigrant. She is complicit in marginalizing him, saying "Just another *brazer* who didn't speak English. Just another wetback." Her language mimics that of the police who question her, mimics that of her cousin as she tries to explain what she was doing out at three in the morning. Esperanza, with her own status as a female immigrant, feels empathy for this man who will quickly be forgotten as he belonged to neither the United States nor Mexico. She imagines his rented flats the and money he sent home—the only tangible evidence he had made it to America. When the money ceases, he will be forgotten. There is no structure in place to identify him or to tell his family he is gone. When the money stops, they will wonder and then agree to give his life over to the country he adopted, ceasing to own any concern for his fate, and so to save him in some small way, Esperanza imagines for him a story. Guitterez-Jones believes "She expresses herself as an artist by expressing the struggles of others, establishing her own identity as she conveys the identity of her neighborhood" (307). Esperanza acted out of empathy and the need to represent those who could no longer represent themselves.

"Edna's Ruthie" is yet another disenfranchised person living in the neighborhood. Though she used to write children's books and was once married, she has returned to her mother in a state of child-like innocence. From Esperanza's point of view she is the only adult she knows who likes to play, and so they play together. Ruthie is the daughter of Edna, the owner of the building next door to Esperanza. She is infamous for her ruthless expulsions of tenants, particularly a pregnant woman she threw out for owning a duck. Esperanza recognizes that Edna would throw Ruthie out as well were she able, but because the young woman is her daughter, she allows her to live there, even though Edna does not show affection to the woman. Esperanza immediately recognizes the difference between familial duty and love, and in some ways tries to compensate for Edna in her treatment of Ruthie. Ruthie will not enter the candy store with the children, instead she stands outside waiting. If she does go inside she gets the look of a trapped animal, suggesting abuse in her past. The children give her candy although her teeth are soft. She keeps saying that she will go to the dentist the next week. She still possesses the inclinations toward adulthood, but is unable to act upon them. Though the children notice, they choose not to call her on the truth of her comments. She also sees lovely things in everything. Ruthie's ability to see the beauty in life attracts Esperanza to her. Sadly, the experience of beauty is tempered by an inability to make decisions. Esperanza relates the story of when Ruthie is asked to go bowling and a car of people wait for her to make a decision. Ruthie panics and asks her mother who tells her she doesn't care what Ruthie does. Ruthie remains incapacitated by indecision until the car finally pulls away. That night in support of the woman, the children ask her to play cards and allow her to deal, a tacit way of indicating their sympathy.

Still, Esperanza, though she totally accepts Ruthie, wonders why anyone would move to Mango Street if they didn't have to, and wonders where the woman's husband is even though Ruthie claims she is only visiting and that he will be coming for her. Though her husband never arrives, Esperanza doesn't judge her. Husband or no, she is a friend and Esperanza chooses to give primacy to that. In fact, she is such a friend that Esperanza shares her books with her and even memorizes an entire poem to recite to her, a gift of great distinction to this child of words. She chooses to recite "The Walrus and the Carpenter" by Lewis Carroll which chronicles the story of the Walrus and the Carpenter duping a group of young oysters to follow them on a walk, after which point the two devour all of the oysters. Perhaps because of the violent nature of this metric poem, at the end of the recitation, Ruthie looks at Esperanza for a long time and then tells her "You have the most beautiful teeth I have ever seen," as if perhaps those teeth might eat her.

Esperanza continues with her neighborhood characters in **"The Earl of Tennessee."** Earl is yet another neighbor who lives in a basement apartment in Edna's building and works nights. He interacts with the children when he tells them to be quiet and when he gives away portions of his massive collection of damp 45's. As with almost all of the characters in the neighborhood, he is reproduced through Esperanza as a combination of good and bad. One of the most remarkable things about the protagonist is her lack of judgment concerning her neighbors. She tells of a wife that Earl is supposed to have and then lists at least three women that the people in the neighborhood suspect is his wife. With each woman, Earl behaves the same: "Whenever she arrives, he holds her tight by the crook of the arm. They walk fast into the apartment, lock the door behind them and don't stay long." As is often the case, Esperanza's voice allows for an objective retelling of significant details counting on the cultural literacy of the readers to put the puzzle together. Earl's "wives" are prostitutes despite the euphemistic term of wife applied by the older generation.

"Sire" marks an important turning point in Esperanza's development. In this chapter, she undergoes a rapid sexual metamorphosis. Suddenly, one day, she notices that a boy named Sire is watching her, and having someone notice her as a sexual being is both thrilling and frightening for her. As she walks past his house, he stares while he "pitches pennies" with his buddies. Esperanza is determined to not be like other girls, she vows instead to be brave and to walk right past him rather than crossing the street. She even dares to glance at him just once to show that she is not afraid, saying "I had to look hard, just once, like he was glass. And I did. I did once." The one time was enough to unsettle her as she stared too long and so transfixed Sire that he rode his bike into a car. She states "It made your blood freeze to have somebody look at you like that." The experience excites her, makes her feel like she is finally becoming a woman because she has been viewed as one by an aroused male. However, she is not the only one aware of Sire's ardor. Esperanza's father calls him a "punk" and her mother tells her not to talk to him.

The problem is quickly solved when Sire's girlfriend arrives. She is a petite, child-like woman to whom Esperanza compares herself. The girl-woman smells like babies, has little painted toes and cannot tie her own shoes. Esperanza feels a brief satisfaction that she at least can tie her own shoes, but the shoe tying is merely a trick to get a man to tie them for her, to kneel at her feet and look up at her and be close to her, to make him feel like her protector. Critic Michelle Scalise Sugiyama views "girl-woman" as agreeing to her own submission based on gender roles; she comments "This is perhaps best illustrated in the relationship between the tellingly named Sire and his girlfriend, 'tiny and pretty' Lois, who is compared to a baby three times in the same paragraph. We are told not that she and Sire hold hands when they go out on walks, but that *she* holds *his* hand, and that they stop periodically for him to tie her shoes. Whether or not Lois is faking this inability to tie her own shoes, the submission and dependence it results in are quite real" (18). However, Esperanza still sees it as titillating and romantic. Sometimes Esperanza hears them at night laughing and says she can hear the "the trees talking to themselves: wait, wait, wait." She is on the brink of falling in love and becoming a fully sexualized being and she watches the couple in fascination, watching to see what will happen to her. The couple leaves for walks together and Esperanza wonders where he takes her. According to her mother it is into an alley. The women in the barrio are sometimes equally complicit in judging a woman based on her sexual behavior and Esperanza's mother is no exception.

Still, the entire relationship and her own sexual identity are unfolding before her eyes and Esperanza can feel everything in her "holding its breath." She says "Everything is waiting to explode like Christmas. I want to be all new and shiny. I want to sit out bad at night, a boy around my neck and the wind under my skirt." Esperanza sees her future if she gives into her urges: she will have a boy and she will have the freedom of the wind in her hair and under her skirt as it were, but she will be classified as bad. She also believes that with these newly found sexual urges she will become a whole new person, as if the first years of her life were simply crystalline years for the divine being she is to become. Still, perhaps being labeled as bad would be better than the intense longing she feels. She whiles away the hours fixating on Sire, embracing and talking to the trees in her yard and imagining what he and his girlfriend are doing.

In **"Four Skinny Trees"** Esperanza pays homage to the trees that constitute her confidantes. She relates to them believing that they, like her, are misplaced in the city. They speak to her at night through the window, but it is a special secret because her sister, Nenny, sleeps through the whispers. In an act of intense identification, Esperanza describes the trees as having secret strength: "They send ferocious roots beneath the ground. They grow up and they grow down and grab the earth between their hairy toes and bite the sky with violent teeth and never quit their anger. This is how they keep." Esperanza admires their fierceness and wants it for herself, a sustaining desire that will help her through her shame of living on Mango Street and maintain her desire for a real house. The trees represent sheer perseverance against the harsh scope of the city. They call to her: "Keep, keep, keep, trees say when I sleep. They teach." Their lesson is determination and when Esperanza fears that she will forget to stay true to this family and their message, she stares at the branches that continue to reach into the sky despite their surroundings.

"No Speak English" is a critical chapter as well, for the way in which Esperanza describes the experience of an immigrant in her neighborhood. Completely contrary to the traditional view of the immigrant striving to come to America in pursuit of the American dream, Mamacita comes because her husband sends for her. In America, he works two jobs, saves his money and sends for his wife and child in Mexico. When they finally come, Esperanza is fascinated by the woman from the start. When Mamacita extends her dainty foot from the cab, its tiny proportions and pink color seem absolutely beautiful even as Esperanza views the thick ankle and finally the entire woman as she is pushed and pulled from the taxi by her husband and the driver. Esperanza describes it, "All at once she bloomed. Huge, enormous, beautiful to look at, from the salmon-pink feather on the tip of her hat to the little rosebuds of her shoes." She makes the woman into a hothouse flower of sorts and the woman fulfils the image because she remains forever in the apartment and forever foreign to the inhabitants of the neighborhood.

Esperanza emphasizes the tiny feet and the unlikely woman that they carry. The eroticized shoes speak again to females being cloistered as Michelle Scalise Sugiyama suggests (12). Some say she doesn't come down from the apartment because she is too fat, others say that she doesn't come down because she cannot descend and then climb the stairs again, but the ever attentive Esperanza believes it is because she can't speak English and without a language, Mamacita will remain forever excluded from her new culture. Esperanza's father reinforces this belief when he remembers that the only words that he spoke when he came to America were "hamandeggs." He ordered it for every meal as it was the only English he knew. When Esperanza says now he no longer has hamandeggs, it is clear that her father has made the crucial linguistic transition necessary to become a public citizen of the United States.

Although Mamacita does not come out, the neighbors know that she is there from her singing homesick songs as she listens to the Spanish radio shows. Her homesickness is so intense that her husband paints the interior of the apartment pink, like the house that she left, but it is not enough. Mamacita is still racked with homesickness. She cries for home and her husband becomes angry and yells at her, telling her that they are home.

Esperanza describes the effect of his words: "¡*A! Mamacita*, who does not belong, every once in a while lets out a cry, hysterical, high, as if he had torn the only skinny thread that kept her alive, the only road to that country." Esperanza describes it so well because she closely associates with Mamacita's feelings of dislocation and powerlessness over her situation. Mamacita is at the mercy of her husband's desires and must live where he dictates. The final nail is hammered into the coffin of Mamacita's new life when her baby boy begins talking and sings the Pepsi commercial he heard on television. Recognizing that her life in Mexico is over, she begs the baby not to become American, not to adopt English, the "tinny, harsh" language. She cries out to him "No, no, no, as if she can't believe her ears."

In **"Rafaela Who Drinks Coconut & Papaya Juice on Tuesdays,"** we see another woman at the mercy of a man. Rafaela gets locked indoors when her husband comes home because he believes she might run away since "she is too beautiful to look at." Clearly her beauty makes her sexual prey and sexually powerful. He seeks to contain that power. As a result, Rafaela must ask the neighborhood kids to get her papaya juice or coconut juice. She sends down the money on a string and the kids return with her request, tie it back to the string and she pulls it up into her room. Rafaela too is displaced from her youth, from dancing and having fun; instead, she leans in the window longing to be independent to "throw green eyes easily like dice and open homes with keys." She believes that with her freedom and her sexual power, life would be better, less bitter. Still the brief vignette ends with the idea of "someone promising to keep them on a silver string." Even her visions of freedom culminate in a man giving her freedom, not in her own self-sufficiency.

"Sally" the title character of this chapte,r is a friend of Esperanza's, a beautiful girl whose father is overbearing in his protection of his daughter's virginity. According to Esperanza, Sally's father claims that "to be this beautiful is trouble," another suggestion that the danger comes from a woman's sexual power and a man's predatory nature. Her father excuses his behavior based on the severity of his religion. He fears that his daughter will become like his sisters, who, it is intimated, fell from grace and shamed the family. However, for Esperanza, Sally is exotic and sexual, someone from whom she might learn to control her own burgeoning sexual power. Esperanza asks questions of Sally about beauty tricks. Unlike Sally, Esperanza has a mother who watches carefully over everything she wears: no nylons, no black shoes, and no make-up. Mrs. Cordero claims that "to wear black so young is dangerous." Again, the notion of danger and sexuality are closely linked.

For Esperanza and for others, Sally proves to be a dangerous friend. Sally loses her best friend after trying to pierce her ears. The incident results in a fight where Sally gets bitten by the friend and called a name. Bravely, Sally refused to cry but Esperanza knows that this loss is a painful one, leaving Sally without someone to confide in and share with. Esperanza's sense of empathy is so intense that she defends Sally in the telling of the story, adamantly stating that the stories the boys tell in the coatroom are not true. Again, the suggestion is that these stories are about Sally's sexual permissiveness and Esperanza chooses to defend her as she sees Sally become two different people between school and the neighborhood. Before Sally goes home, she wipes off her make-up and straightens her skirt, becoming the perfect daughter for her father who locks her in the house. Esperanza wonders if Sally ever wishes she didn't have to go home, if the girl ever wants to move to another house. Esperanza's platonic crush on Sally has her projecting her own desires onto Sally. Suddenly in her attempt to articulate Sally's desire, she is articulating her own:

> There'd be no nosy neighbors watching, no motorcycles and cars, no sheets and towels and laundry. Only trees and more trees and plenty of blue sky. And you could laugh, Sally. You could go to sleep and wake up and never have to think of who likes and doesn't like you. You could close your eyes and you wouldn't have to worry what people said because you never belonged here anyway and nobody could make you sad and nobody would think you're

strange because you like to dream and dream. And no one could yell at you if they saw you out in the dark leaning against a car, leaning against somebody without someone thinking you are bad, without somebody saying it is wrong, without the whole world waiting for you to make a mistake when all you wanted, all you wanted, Sally, was to love and to love and to love and to love, and no one could call that crazy. (83)

In this moment of reverie, Esperanza expresses all of the things that she feels imprison her on Mango Street: the environment itself, the repressive social code, the nosy neighbors, the lack of dreams, the suffocating gender stratification that labels sexual women bad and the lack of openness. Guiterrez-Jones asserts "In particular, Esperanza grasps Sally's unhappiness, and shares with her the anguish of a home that can never fulfill that term's promise—a home which is not her own, a home where 'she never belonged ... anyway'" (304). On a technical note, the rhythm that Cisneros builds directly mirrors the rhythms of Esperanza's desire.

In **"Minerva Writes Poems"** Esperanza sees to a certain degree how the desire for a man too early can result in a life of misery. Minerva is only a little older than Esperanza herself but she has two children, an unstable marriage and an abusive husband. Esperanza and Minerva exchange poems with each other. Minerva fits her creative life in around her children and her husband, a caution to Esperanza who wants to give her writing primacy in life. Writing is becoming, as Elenita the witch woman foretold, the home within her heart. Minerva's marriage also enhances Esperanza's wariness of men as Minerva's husband "who left and keeps leaving" returns home to find all of his stuff thrown out of the house. He beats his wife in response, then apologizes and she lets him back in. Esperanza watches Minerva enact the abused wife syndrome, allowing her husband and the suffering he brings with him, to rule both her actual and creative life. After her husband returns, she asks Esperanza "what can (I) do?" Esperanza is defeated by the situation, unable to help her friend and unable to foresee what will happen in Minerva's future. She finished the chapter saying "There is nothing I can do." Esperanza has given up on helping Minerva who has given up on saving herself. They are both worn down by the circumstances.

Still, Esperanza maintains her desire to help people despite her experience with Minerva. In **"Bums in the Attic"** she explains the humanitarian portion of her fantasy house based on Sunday drives she took with her family to look at the gardens of the rich people for whom her father works. When she announces that she no longer wants to go on these rides her father assumes it is because she is "getting too old" for it. Her sister Nenny suggests it is because Esperanza is "getting too stuck up. "What Esperanza doesn't tell them is that she is ashamed, "all of us staring out the window like the hungry. I'm tired of looking at what we can't have. When we win the lottery ... Mama begins, and then I stop listening." Esperanza feels distanced from her family and disillusioned, too old to believe in the family dream of the lottery or some other divine intervention. She realizes that whatever comes to them must be earthbound, from the hard work or generosity of one committed person. When she looks at the houses on the hills, she recognizes that the people who live in those houses are too content to look at what other people need, that they fear nothing and know nothing of what goes on in the neighborhoods below them. Their willful ignorance makes Esperanza vow: "One day I'll own my own house, but I won't forget who I am or where I came from." She determines to let passing bums have the attic of her house, where they will be safe. She will do this because she will always remember what it means to have the house and to have gone without the house. She envisions herself sitting by the fire with guests and explaining the creaking floorboards to friends, "Bums, I'll say and I'll be happy."

Esperanza continues to blaze her own path of liberation in **"Beautiful and Cruel."** She names herself the ugly daughter, the one "nobody comes for." It is the beauty of the woman, she believes, that makes the suitor come to take the woman away. Her sister Nenny on the other hand is pretty. Nenny says that "she won't wait her whole life for a husband to come and get her." The girl notes that a neighbor left Mango Street by having a baby, but Nenny doesn't want that either. She wants to pick and choose her mate. Esperanza thinks it is easy for Nenny to make these decisions because her younger sister is the pretty sort of girl that men desire. Esperanza's mother notices her older daughter's jealousy and tells her that when she gets older her "dusty hair will settle" and her "blouse will learn to stay clean," but even in the midst of this reassurance, Esperanza remains unconvinced that this is actually what she wants. Rather, she vows "not to grow up tame like the others who lay their necks on the threshold waiting for the ball and chain." She decides that whatever fate she has, she will be in control of it. She thinks of movies where "there is always one with red red lips who is beautiful and cruel." This woman controls the men around her with her sexuality and she refuses to give that power away. Esperanza chooses to be that woman, to take control of her power. She begins her campaign quietly, by leaving "the table like a man, without putting back the chair or picking up the plate." She realizes that to have power, she has to take it and actively choose to break gender codes, and she begins with the table.

To further illustrate the purpose of her battle, Esperanza explains the regrets of her mother in **"A Smart Cookie."** Her mother laments what she might have been if she hadn't given in to cultural norms and gotten married and pregnant. Her mother is multi-talented: she sings opera, knows how to fix the television, speaks two languages, makes beautiful pieces with needle and thread, but is unable to function outside of the barrio. The city, though she has lived there her whole life, defeats and intimidates her. Though she wants to see a play, a ballet, an opera, she does nothing to create these experiences for herself, but instead lives vicariously by singing along with opera albums borrowed from the library. What is perhaps most moving about Mrs. Cordero is that she knows she has given up her life. She tells her daughter to study hard and to rely solely on herself, citing other women whose husbands have left, leaving them with nothing. She says, "Got to take care all your own." Then she follows her outburst with a few last words, explaining to Esperanza that she left school due to shame over her old clothes. She urges her daughter to not accept shame but to rise above it and choose her life, rather than choosing to be subjugated based on public opinion.

The thread of the abusive male continues in **"What Sally Said."** The chapter begins with Sally rationalizing her father's abuse, "He never hits me hard." Regardless of her claim, her mother has to rub the places it hurts with lard and Sally has to lie about the abuse when she goes to school, claiming she fell to explain all of the bruises and scars. No one, particularly not Esperanza, is fooled. Sally is too old to be so clumsy and the claim that he never hits her hard lies in direct opposition to her swollen and bruised face. One day, as Sally describes it, "he hit her with his hands just like a dog." According to Sally his motivation stems from the fact that she is a daughter, who might run away like his own sisters did, thereby shaming the family. After this incident, Sally gets permission to stay with Esperanza's family. She brings with her some clothes and a pathetic offering of a sweetbread from her powerless mother. That night her father comes to the house, fresh from weeping to beg his daughter to come home, claiming it won't happen again. Then, Esperanza believes there is nothing more to worry about until a few days later, when Sally's father sees her talking to a boy. Over the next few days, Sally doesn't come to school. Her father beat her with his belt, "[U]ntil the way Sally tells it, he just went crazy, he just forgot he was her father between the buckle and the belt." Afterwards he repeats to himself "You're not my daughter, you're not my daughter" and then weeps. It is hard to tell if part of his self-loathing is based on sexual abuse or if it is solely physical abuse. In either case, he reinforces the pattern of men and violence, particularly within domestic spaces.

Sally is in trouble again in **"The Monkey Garden"** but this time the trouble is of her own making. The monkey garden was formerly inhabited by a family with a mean monkey that bit and screeched. Once the family left, the children of the neighborhood begin to take over the garden as a place to play, imagining that it had been there since time began. Within a few months after the former tenants move out, the garden begins to reclaim itself, growing over bricks and boundaries. Cars were left there mysteriously and the garden grew over them as well. This wild abundance in some ways easily figures as the Garden of Eden, particularly with the sexual awakening that is going to happen there. Esperanza plays with the other children, climbing through the cars until she realizes that Sally is missing. When she goes to look for her friend, she sees that Tito and his friends have stolen Sally's keys and have conceived of a game wherein they will only return the keys to her if she kisses them. Immediately, Esperanza knows that this is a dangerous game, though she can't articulate exactly what she objects to, something in her knows that bartering sexual favors is not right. In her panic, she runs up to Tito's apartment and tells his mother who laughs it off as childish mischief. Determined to save her friend on her own, Esperanza gathers three sticks and a brick to beat the boys off, convinced that Sally wants to be saved from the power-mongering boys.

When Esperanza arrives on the scene with her arsenal, Sally tells her to go home. The boys tell her to leave them alone, and Esperanza feels absolute shame over what the other adolescents have made her feel is her over-reaction. She hides herself in the jungle of the monkey garden, to cry out of sight. Her shame is so great that she tries to will her heart to stop beating like the Indian priests she has read about. The event causes Esperanza to lose the garden. Like the Garden of Eden, the entrance of knowledge has caused it to be lost forever, only in this role reversal, Esperanza is the Adamic character seduced by her friendship with Sally into uncovering knowledge she doesn't really want. Critic Ellen McCracken links this story with others ("What Sally Said," "Red Clowns") in what she deems the "Sally cycle" in which Esperanza begins to make powerful connections between "sex, male power, and violence in patriarchal society" (69).

In **"Red Clowns"** Sally again causes hurt to Esperanza. In the beginning of the chapter, Esperanza sounds desperate and betrayed, insisting "Sally, you lied. It wasn't what you said at all. What he did. Where he touched me. I didn't want it, Sally. The way they said it, the way it's supposed to be, all the storybooks and movies, why did you lie to me?" Esperanza is sexually assaulted by a older boy at the fairly which defames her bookish ideas of love and sexual pleasure. At the heart of the assault is Sally who was supposed to meet Esperanza by the clowns but fails to do so. Esperanza waits, wondering where the big boy that Sally left with has taken her. While waiting for her friend, a group of boys approaches Esperanza, one grabs her arm and says "I love you, Spanish girl, I love you." His use of her ethnicity to name her suggests that he is white. The boys sexually assault her and Esperanza is powerless to do anything but scream until eventually she can only cry. She feels betrayed on multiple levels by Sally who doesn't come to save her, by all of the lies that she has heard about sexual pleasure, by waiting her whole life for a moment that turns out to be both painful and ugly. Critic Maria Herrera-Sobek articulates the betrayal in terms of the community:

> The diatribe is directed not only at Sally the silent interlocutor but at the community of women who keep the truth from the younger generation of women in a conspiracy of silence. The protagonist discovers a conspiracy of two forms of silence: silence in not denouncing the "real" facts of life about sex and its negative aspects in violent sexual encounters, and complicity in embroidering a fairy-tale-like mist around sex, and romanticizing and idealizing unrealistic sexual relations (252).

The effect of silence is part of Esperanza's shame and need to deny the assault when she begs Sally not to make her tell the whole of what happened. All of Esperanza's innocent pleasure in her sexual awakening is shattered in this moment and her friendship with Sally is irrevocably destroyed.

"Linoleum Roses" documents the seemingly inevitable. Sally gets married to a salesman she meets at the school bazaar and moves to another state where it is legal to get married before the eighth grade. Sally claims to be happy because she can buy things now, but her husband has violent tendencies like her father and though she claims that she left for love, Esperanza believes she married the salesman to escape. Her husband keeps Sally locked tight in the house. She cannot look out the window or talk on the telephone and friends are not allowed to visit unless he is away. In the final moment of the chapter, Sally sits inside the house looking at all of the things that they own, never realizing that she is an owned thing among them.

In **"The Three Sisters,"** Cisneros writes of three elderly aunts from Mexico. Critic Maria Elena de Valdes links them to a number of traditions:

> In pre-Hispanic Mexico, the lunar goddesses, such as Tlazolteotl and Xochiquetzal, were the intermediaries for all women (Westheim 105). They are sisters to each other and, as women, sisters to Esperanza ... At the symbolic level, the sisters are linked with Clotho, Lachesis, and Atropos, the three fates ... In Cisneros's text, the prophecy of the fates turn to the evocation of self-knowledge. (58)

The revelatory women are great aunts of Lucy and Rachel's and they come after the death of the girl's baby sibling. The child dies after a series of signs: a dog's cry and bird flying into an open window. At the funeral, everyone comes to look at the house and to pray for the baby who Esperanza describes as "that little thumb of a human in a box like candy." For Esperanza, the rituals of the wake are new and unsettling. As she stands in the room uncertain of what to do, the three old sisters call her over to them. Esperanza feels trepidation but relaxes when she pinpoints their collective scent as that of "Kleenex or the inside of a satin handbag." The three sisters ask Esperanza her name and she answers them. One of the sisters comments that Esperanza's name is "good," another says that her knees hurt, it will rain tomorrow. Esperanza wants to know how they can predict this weather and the women never blame it on arthritis, they simply say, "We know." Then they look at her hands and become animated, murmuring among themselves that Esperanza will "go very far." They tell the girl to make a wish. Esperanza asks to make sure there are no limits to this wish, and they assure her there are not, she immediately wishes for her own house. When she is finished the women assure her that it will come true. Again, Esperanza asks how they know, and they reiterate, "We know, we know." Then, the woman with the marble hands pulls Esperanza aside, takes her face between her palms and tells her "When you leave you must remember to always come back." Immediately, Esperanza is baffled and a little afraid, believing the woman has read her mind. The old woman repeats, "When you leave you must remember to come back for the others. A circle, understand? You will always be Esperanza. You will always be Mango Street. You can't erase what you know. You can't forget who you are." Esperanza is both spooked and speechless from the woman's insight. The old woman continues, explaining that others will not be able to leave as easily as she, that she must respect them and come back to help. Esperanza promises to remember and the old lady dismissed Esperanza to go play with Lucy and Rachel. To enhance the strangeness and portent of the experience, she never sees the women again.

The women become, in their own way, members of the circle of women that surround Esperanza. These women encourage her with words, like her mother, Ruthie and Aunt Lupe, they teach through example like Sally, Alicia, and Minerva, they share experience like Minerva, Mamacita, Lucy, and Rachel and they offer futures like Elenita. Within this circle, Esperanza becomes the conduit for their stories and their wisdom. Like many Chicanas, she carries the history of the community with her and learns from it. She also bears witness to the people of Mango Street.

In **"Alicia and I Talking on Edna's Steps"** she gains yet a little more insight. Alicia gives Esperanza a bag from her home, Guadalajara, which she treasures. Alicia's dream is the opposite of Esperanza's. She does not want to move towards a place unknown, she wants to return to the place that she knows best, her home in Mexico. Esperanza confides in Alicia her disappointment over not having a house. A little baffled, Alicia points to the house on Mango Street, asking Esperanza whether or not this is her home. Esperanza denies it is her own: "No this isn't my house I say and shake my head as if shaking could undo the year I've lived here. I don't belong. I don't ever want to come from here." Desperate to be understood, she invokes Alicia's situation of having a home to return to where she can be happy and can belong. Alicia forces her to face the reality: "No, Alicia says. Like it or not you are Mango Street and one day you'll come back too." Esperanza denies, saying she won't come back until Mango Street is better. Alicia laughs at the idea, wondering who would ever try to make it better, emphasizing again how forgotten and disenfranchised the neighborhood really is. She and Esperanza joke that maybe the mayor will do it, but the conversation sets Esperanza into wondering who will come to Mango Street. She is slowly coming to believe that the duty may perhaps fall to her. McCracken links this discussion to Esperanza's comments on bums in the attic: "She conceives of a house as a communal rather than private property; such sharing runs counter to the dominant ideological discourse that strongly affects consciousness in capitalist societies." (64) Again, the emphasis on the individual is minimal compared to the communal whole.

In the next chapter, **"A House of My Own"** there is a sense of lineage between Esperanza's chapter and Virginia Woolf's *A Room of One's Own*. Both women are fighting to have space for their writing and a right to their lives. Esperanza dreams of a house that is not a flat or an apartment, and that more importantly is "Not a man's house. Not a daddy's," instead it is one that is only hers. Guitterez-Jones sees this as a rejection of male traditions, critic and Jacqueline Doyle believes the desire is in keeping with Virginia Woolf's desire for *A Room of One's Own*. Esperanza determines to make the house beautiful with flowers and books, where her things stay where they are left and no one interferes or judges her decisions. She wants "Only a house quiet as snow, a space for myself to go, clean as paper before the poem." Each item in her list references the notion of possibility. With this house, she will have the opportunity to do whatever she would like, unlike the barrio where the opportunities are limited by income, by gender, by language and by ethnicity.

In the final chapter of the book, **"Mango Says Goodbye Sometimes,"** nearly a year after the beginning, Esperanza has finally begun to build the house of the heart that Elenita foretold in her kitchen. Esperanza writes about how she likes to tell stories, to narrate her own life as she lives it. She begins to tell the story of her house on Mango Street, returning to some of the language that began the book. The act of writing frees Esperanza from the memory of the house where she belongs but does "not belong to." Writing allows her to say good-bye to Mango Street, to release the ghost of her past. These first pages of her story tell her that she will be able to eventually say good-bye to Mango and leave forever. She imagines her friends and neighbors gossiping and wondering where it is she has gone and why she has to go so far away. Esperanza keeps the secret of her strength, "They will not know I have gone away to come back. For the ones I left behind. For the ones who cannot get out." Esperanza must find the place and privacy within her where she can write and free herself from the memory of Mango and in so doing, she will liberate the others by telling their stories. Critic Yvonne Yarbro-Bejarano defines what will become Esperanza's legacy: "Writing has been essential in connecting her with the power of women and her promise to pass down that power to other women is fulfilled by the writing and the publication of the text itself" (217). The very act of circling back to the language of the beginning of the book suggests that Esperanza has, in fact, begun to bring the story to paper and obviously to print. This self-conscious move reinforces the act of writing as a mode of bearing witness for the disenfranchised who appear throughout *The House on Mango Street*.

Works Cited

De Valdés, Maria Elena. "In Search of Identity in Cisneros's *The House on Mango Street*." *Canadian Review of American Studies* 23:1 (Fall 1992).

Gutiérrez-Jones, Leslie S. "Different Voices: The Re-Bildung of the Barrio in Sandra Cisneros' *The House of Mango Street.*" *Anxious Power: Reading, Writing, and in Narrative by Women.* Eds. Carol J. Singley and Susan Elizabeth Sweeney. Albany: State University of New York Press, 1993.

Herrera-Sobek, María "The Politics of Rape: Sexual Transgression in Chicana Fiction." *Chicana Creativity and Criticism: New Frontiers in American Literature, 2nd Ed.* Eds. María Herrera-Sobek and Helena María Viramontes. Albuquerque: University of New Mexico Press, 1996.

Kuribayashi, Tomoko. "The Chicana Girl Writes Her Way In and Out: Space and Bilingualism in Sandra Cisneros' *The House on Mango Street.*" *Creating Safe Spaces: Violence and Women's Writings.* Eds. Tomoko Kuribayashi and Julie Tharpe. Albany: State University of New York Press: 1998.

McCracken, Ellen. "Sandra Cisneros' *The House on Mango Street*: Community-Oriented Introspection and the Demystification of Patriarchal Violence." *Breaking Boundaries: Latina Writing and Critical Readings,* eds. Asunción Horno-Delgado, Eliana Ortega, Nina M. Scott and Nancy Saporta Sternbach. Amherst: The University of Massachusetts Press, 1989.

Olivares, Julián "Sandra Cisneros' *House on Mango Street* and the Poetics of Space." *Chicana Creativity and Criticism: New Frontiers in American Literature, 2nd Ed.* Eds. María Herrera-Sobek and Helena María Viramontes. Albuquerque: University of New Mexico Press, 1996.

Sugiyama, Michelle Scalise. "Of Woman Bondage: The Eroticism of Feet in *The House on Mango Street.*" *The Midwest Quarterly* 41:1 (Autumn 1999).

Yarbro-Bejarano Yvonne. "Chicana Literature from a Chicana Feminist Perspective." *Chicana Creativity and Criticism: New Frontiers in American Literature, 2nd Ed.* Eds. María Herrera-Sobek and Helena María Viramontes. Albuquerque: University of New Mexico Press, 1996.

Critical Views

JODY NORTON ON HISTORY, REMEMORY, AND TRANSFORMATION

Sandra Cisneros's *The House on Mango Street* is a book about growing up in a Chicago barrio. Told through the naive but perceptive eyes of Esperanza, it consists of a series of character studies and vignettes through which the people of the neighborhood, their lives and problems, and especially their gender roles and relations, are revealed.

In "The Monkey Garden," the neighborhood children move into a marvelous play space previously inhabited by a monkey in a cage and his Kentuckian keepers. The garden is a timeless, borderless Neverland into which "Things had a way of disappearing," "Far away from where our mothers could find us" (95). One day, however, Esperanza's friend Sally will no longer run with her "up and down and through the monkey garden, fast as the boys" (96):

> I said, Sally, come on, but she wouldn't. She stayed by the curb talking to Tito and his friends. Play with the kids if you want, she said, I'm staying here. (96)

Esperanza returns to find that Tito and his friends are playing a new kind of game with Sally. They won't return her keys unless she goes into the garden with them, and gives each of them a kiss.

Esperanza reports the impending assault, as she perceives it, to Tito's mother, but failing to arouse her concern, grabs a brick and decides to rescue her friend herself. The concluding passage of "The Monkey Garden" reads as follows:

> But when I got there Sally said go home. Those boys said, leave us alone. I felt stupid with my brick. They all looked at me as if I was the one that was crazy and made me feel ashamed.

And then I don't know why but I had to run away. I had
to hide myself at the other end of the garden, in the
jungle part, under a tree that wouldn't mind if I lay down
and cried a long time. I closed my eyes like tight stars so
that I wouldn't, but I did. My face felt hot. Everything
inside hiccupped.

I read somewhere in India there are priests who can
will their heart to stop beating. I wanted to will my blood
to stop, my heart to quit its pumping. I wanted to be
dead, to turn into the rain, my eyes melt into the ground
like two black snails. I wished and wished. I closed my
eyes and willed it, but when I got up my dress was green
and I had a headache.

I looked at my feet in their white socks and ugly round
shoes. They seemed far away. They didn't seem to be my
feet anymore. And the garden that had been such a good
place to play didn't seem mine either. (97–98)

Loneliness, according to Harry Stack Sullivan, "is the most
painful of human experiences" (Greenberg 93). Yet the
experience of exclusion and pain here is only partly about the
loss of a friend. More importantly, as Esperanza's projective
identification with her feet shows, it is about the loss of her
childhood self.

The child does grow up, and the world she discovers, with
its ingrown patterns of domination and abuse, most often feels
less like a gift than like a tragic loss. Because most of us have
our own memories of a moment when our preadolescent reality
seemed suddenly to have shifted to one side without telling
us—at which we felt indignant, betrayed, shamed, and
isolated—it is easy for us to engage Cisneros's poignant
(because simple and frank) account, and to make literary
experience through the intertextual relation of Cisneros's
fiction and our own emotional past. The fact that Cisneros
creates a childish yet selective, emotive yet imagistically distinct
voice for Esperanza facilitates our imaginative engagement.
The representation of ego-splitting in the last paragraph, in
which Esperanza's feet seem far away and not hers, is

particularly powerful, because it locates a crucial psychostructural moment—the moment when Esperanza stops being a child—that can resonate with an analogous moment in the reader's history.

The House on Mango Street is a book about a woman writing, a woman enacting the politics of *A Room of One's Own*, but without the class privilege of Woolf. Writing is both Esperanza's mode of struggle and her means of constructing the self she needs to become. "I make a story for my life," she tells us, "about a girl who didn't want to belong" (109). "You must keep writing," Esperanza's dying Aunt Guadalupe admonishes her, "It will keep you free" (61). "The Monkey Garden" calls on us to rememorate—to rewrite and reunderstand—the pain of exclusion, the anger, the lost self-esteem, and to become newly aware of the value both of self-definition and of connection—here the fragile strength of women's connections with each other, in resistance to male oppression—as we experience our own identificatory connection with Esperanza. She is, through responsive reading, both our friend and ourself.

Maria Elena De Valdés on Esperanza's Search for Identity

The poetic text cannot operate if we separate the speaker from her language; they are the inseparable unity of personal identity. There is no utterance before enunciation. There is a fictional persona, Esperanza Cordero, who will speak, and there is the implicit continued use of idiomatic American English. But the enunciation that we read is at once the speaker and the spoken which discloses the subject, her subjectivity, and ours. An inescapable part of this subject is what she is expected to be: "Mexicans, don't like their women strong" (12). "I wonder if she [my great-grandmother] made the best with what she got or was she sorry because she couldn't be all the things she wanted to be. Esperanza. I have inherited her name, but I don't want to inherit her place by the window" (12). This close reading of the text with attention to how it operates, suggests a movement and a counter-movement which I have described metaphorically as the movement of a loom weaving the presence of subjectivity. Subjectivity is always seen against the background of her community that is Chicago's changing neighbourhoods. This determinate background gives narrative continuation, or narrativity, to the narrator's thoughts. The narrative development of this text can be described as the elaboration of the speaker's subjectivity. The symbolic space she creates should not be abstracted from the writing, because the writing itself is the creation of her own space.[6] The structure of this text, therefore, begins as a frame for self-invention and as the writing progresses so does the subject. She is, in the most direct sense of the word, making herself and in a space of her own.

There are numerous empirical and verisimilar truth-claims about the way of life in the neighbourhood.[7] All of these references form a well-knit web of specific truth-claims about social reality. Simultaneous to these truth claims is another kind of reference. The reference to the narrator's own sense of the world, her wonderment and search for answers of why things are the way they are for her and for those who are her family, friends, and neighbours: Minerva "comes over black and blue and asks what can she do? Minerva. I don't know which way she'll go. There is nothing *I* can do" (80); "Sally. What do you think about when you close your eyes like that? ... Do you wish your feet would one day keep walking and take you far away from Mango Street, far away and maybe your feet would stop in front of a house, a nice one with flowers and big windows" (78). Esperanza meditates after her Aunt Lupe's death: "Maybe she was ashamed. Maybe she was embarrassed it took so many years. The kids who wanted to be kids instead of washing dishes and ironing their papa's shirts, and the husband who wanted a wife again. And then she died, my aunt who listened to my poems. And then we began to dream the dreams" (57). This quest for answers takes on an explicit tension because of the depth of the themes the narrator treats, but the manner in which she develops her search for answers is the fundamental dialectic of self-world. She describes what is around her, she responds to people and places, but, most importantly, she reflects on a world she did not make, and cannot change, but must control or she will be destroyed. She is a young, dark-skinned girl of Mexican parentage, born in Chicago, speaking English, and feeling alienated.

The use of these determinate features is of primary importance, for it is through the interplay between the lyrical introspection and the truth-claims that the fusion of self (enunciating voice) and person (character) takes place. The power of the text lies precisely in the creation of this presence. It is this human presence that transcends the time, place, and condition of the composition to create a literary metaphor for a woman coming of age. Readers halfway around the world, who have never seen Chicago and have never experienced what it is to live with the fear expressed in "All brown all around, we are safe," can, nevertheless, understand what it is to be lonely and alienated and how difficult it is to come out free from an environment that enslaves.

Notes

6. I find it essential to repeat that the critical strategy that effaces the female signature of a text is nothing less than the continuation of a patriarchal tradition of appropriation of the female's work through the destruction of her signature. Cisneros has created a female voice who writes with strength in a social context where doing so is an act of transgression, and she writes for "A las mujeres/To the Women" as the dedication so poignantly states. I want to acknowledge the importance of Nancy K. Miller's article which has offered me the intellectual support for my recasting of text as texture.

7. I had occasion to have a second interview with Cisneros in Tijuana, Mexico, on 12 May 1989, at which time I asked her about the specific references to streets and establishments in Chicago. She said that Mango Street itself is a fictional composite of many streets and places. The references to other streets like Loomis, the church, businesses, etc., are referentially specific to Chicago in the sixties.

For Esperanza, religion is a cultural thing; in her Catholic world, God the father and Virgin Mother are household terms. But for this young poet, religion takes on mythic or poetic dimensions. She sees herself, for instance, as a red "balloon tied to an anchor" (9), as if to say she needs to transcend present conditions where mothers are trapped and fathers abusive. She even sees herself molested in a monkey garden (a modern Eden) among red clowns (bloodthirsty males). She appeals to Aunt Lupe (Guadalupe, after the Mexican Virgin Mother), who tells her to write, to create. In the end, when Esperanza meets three aunts, or sisters (her trinity), she in effect has a spiritual vision, one which she describes in concrete language. One is cat-eyed, another's hands are like marble, a third smells like Kleenex. The girl uses these sights, smells, and touches to envision poetically her future house. As with Huck and Holden, there is something she does not fully understand. What she knows is that through these *comadres* (co-mothers) she will give birth to something very new. Like the two male protagonists, she longs for a respect and compassion absent in her experiences on Mango Street, and these women are her spiritual inspiration.

The ending of *Mango Street* is also very significant in terms of literary continuity. Just prior to the end Esperanza meets the three aunts at the funeral of a sister of her friends Lucy and Rachel; they tell her she cannot forget who she is and that if she leaves she must come back. In the end the girl recognizes that she both belongs and does not belong to Mango street. Then she vows to return to the house because of the "ones who cannot" leave. One reason for this is her writing, which has made her strong. She plans to "put it down on paper and then the ghost does not ache so much" (110). What this means relative to other women's novels is that she reverses a trend. In *Our Nig*, Nig is dissipated in the end. The protagonist of *Yellow Wallpaper* goes crazy before literally crawling over her dominating husband's body. Edna in *The Awakening* swims to her death rather than face a culture that will not recognize her identity. Not so with Esperanza. She is strong (something Mexican women should not be), perfectly aware of the problems with a patriarchal culture, and because of her love for her people, albeit abused and dehumanized, vows to return, and it is the writing which gives her the strength.

Here is where Cisneros returns to Huck and Holden for her cue. Consciously or not, Huck has challenged the very basis of a pre-Civil War culture. In the last fifth of the novel, however, it's not clear whether he returns to the ways of Tom Sawyer in staging Jim's escape or whether he's come to a new level of consciousness where he confronts Tom in the name of Jim. In the end he lights out into the territory so, in his words, they won't "civilize me" (274). In this way he seems to reject the culture of slavery, even though in *Tom Sawyer Among the Indians*, written afterwards, Huck returns to that culture by adopting with Tom old romantic ways. In any case, the notion of going back, even to join an abusive culture, or not going back, is a key issue in Twain's handling of Huck in *The Adventures of Huckleberry Finn*.

Holden is slightly different. In the end he is recovering from the shock he received from living in a post-World War II world. It has devastated him. But in telling his story he seems to come back to normal, so that the very telling has the effect of giving him strength. Indeed, he says,

> I sort of *miss* everybody I told about. Even old Stradlater and Ackley, for instance. I think I even miss that goddam Maurice. (214)

It's not clear how Holden will relate to his phony world again, any more than it is with Huck, except that he consciously chooses it, perhaps because he needs people, no matter what they are like. But the fact is he's going back. Esperanza's choice has a different twist. Thoroughly aware of the abusive nature of her culture, she comes to the decision that though she does not want to come from Mango Street, and does not want to go back till somebody "makes it better" (107), she nevertheless chooses to return for the sake of the others. She is "strong"

(110) and, in contrast to Huck, feels drawn back, not just because she needs people, like Holden, but because, they need her.

MICHELLE SCALISE SUGIYAMA ON THE EROTICISM OF FEET

A discussion of female power might seem out of place in a text which focuses primarily on the rigid control of women by men. However, even in a relentlessly patriarchal society, women have a power over men which only the aging process can take away: the power to sexually arouse. That the girls are at least subconsciously aware of the power the female physique has over the male libido is apparent in their deceptively innocent conversations: "You need them [hips] to dance" (49) says Lucy, to which Esperanza responds, "I don't care what kind I get. Just as long as I get hips" (51). And when Esperanza points out that you need hips to have children, Rachel cautions, "But don't have too many or your behind will spread" (50). The girls have observed this power in others and want it for themselves. In a reference to the precocious Sally, Esperanza's mother warns that "to wear black so young is dangerous" (82), but Esperanza wishes that she could wear shoes like Sally's "black ones made out of suede" (82) and wear "nylons the color of smoke" (81).

This power is ultimately a trap for the women of Mango Street, however, and this is illustrated through Cisneros's use of the shoe motif—most notably through the use of high heels. The effect that high heels have on the gait is not unlike the effect of footbinding, a practice notorious as an expression of male subjugation of women. Anyone who has ever worn high heels knows that they are uncomfortable at best and painful at worst; they slow the gait and make it virtually impossible to run. Overton inadvertently makes the connection between these distinct cultural practices quite clear in the observation that sparked this rumination: "High heels must have been a man's idea—'Their asses will look good *and* they'll be crippled!'" The responses of men to an attractive woman in high heels and to an attractive woman with bound feet are quite similar; indeed, the erotic appeal of bound feet is well documented. In her essay "The Bride-Show Custom and the Fairy-Story of Cinderella," Photeine Bourboulis cites the Chinese tale of "Miss A-pao," which features a beautiful young woman surrounded by a ring of admirers at a spring festival. The admirers' excitement intensifies as she stands up to leave, after which, Bourboulis emphasizes, the men "criticized her face and *discussed her feet*" (105). H.A. Giles, in his book *The Civilization of China*, observes that "any Chinaman will bear witness as to the seductive effect of a gaily dressed girl picking her way on tiny feet some three inches in length, her swaying movements and delightful appearance of instability, conveying a general sense of delicate grace quite beyond expression in words" (106).

Part of the appeal of bound feet is that, as Giles mentions, their growth is retarded, which dramatically decreases their length. High heels, too, cause the foot to appear smaller. Significantly, along with shoes, small feet are a recurring motif in *The House On Mango Street*. The first thing that is mentioned of Mamacita's physical appearance is her "tiny pink shoe" (76). An entire chapter is devoted to a "Family of Little Feet." And Esperanza's shame and embarrassment at having to wear *chanclas* with her new party dress is expressed as a feeling of "My feet growing bigger and bigger" and "My feet swell[ing] big and heavy like plungers" (47). On Mango Street, as in old China, female beauty is associated with foot size: because they make her feet feel large and clumsy, Esperanza feels "ugly" (47) in the *chanclas*.

An appearance of airy gracefulness is another of the appeals of bound feet mentioned by Giles: footbinding causes a woman to sway from side to side as she walks. High heels cause a similar swaying—"tee-tottering" (40) is the word Esperanza uses, which suggests the "appearance of instability" Giles refers to. No doubt the "delightful" effect this "appearance of instability" has on the male psyche is due to the actual instability caused. A crippled woman is easier to control than a woman with healthy limbs. Esperanza unconsciously senses the link between high heels and footbinding: in "My Name" she observes that she was born in "the Chinese year of the horse—which is supposed to be bad luck if you're born female—but I think this is a Chinese lie because the Chinese, like the Mexicans, don't like their women strong" (10).

Footbinding was practiced, of course, for precisely this reason: to make women weak. By making women physically unstable, men were able to curtail their movement and thereby prevent their sisters, wives, and daughters from engaging in any pre- and/or extra-marital sexual activity. As Laura Betzig suggests, "sexual modesty among women, including such strict institutions as veiling, footbinding, and claustration, might function to raise the paternal confidence of their consorts" (8; see also Dickemann). "Girls are like gold, like gems," says a Chinese interviewee to Giles at the turn of the century. "They ought to stay in their own house. If their feet are not bound they go here and they go there with unfitting associates; they have no good name. They are like defective gems that are rejected" (79). A woman whose feet were bound could not walk very far or for a sustained period of time, and had to be transported from place to place via palanquin. "Chinese ladies not walk abroad like Americans," says a Chinese woman interviewed by an American journalist in 1914. "In streets they go in sedan chairs, always with chaperone." This same woman was able to walk alone only with the aid of tables and chairs (Headland, 288). Thus a foot-bound woman was virtually a home-bound woman; for all practical purposes, she was cloistered.

LESLIE S. GUTIÉRREZ-JONES ON THE RE-BUILDING OF THE BARRIO

As narrator, Esperanza creates and chronicles her developing identity not through self-absorbed introspection, but by noting, recording, and responding to the lives around her—those lives for whom almost half of the collection's forty-four "prose poems" are named, and whose significance is underscored by Cisneros' title, which situates Esperanza not as a solitary loner but as she comes to perceive herself: a product and member of a particular community. Immune to the "privilege of power" associated with glorifying the individual, Esperanza comes to understand that the three strange sisters, and her friend Alicia, are right: Mango may say "goodbye *sometimes*," but even when set free from the physical locale, Esperanza "will *always* be Mango Street" (101, 98, my emphases). Protagonists like Cisneros' might be outsiders vis à vis the dominant culture, yet they are emphatically not loners. Unlike the traditional "American"[8] hero, who underscores his independence by isolating himself on the high seas (Captain Ahab), in the wilderness (Thoreau), in the "territories" (Huck Finn), or on the road (Jack Kerouac), Cisneros' hero has no such choice. Esperanza has already been symbolically cast out of mainstream "American" suburbia; her status as outsider is not chosen, but imposed. Yet she does not react to her exteriority by perceiving herself as "alone against the world." Rather, Esperanza defines herself as a member of a community—the community that is Mango Street.

> Let one forget his reason for being, they'd all droop like tulips in a glass, each with their arms around the other. Keep, keep, keep, trees say when I sleep. They teach.
>
> —Sandra Cisneros, *The House on Mango Street*

The reconceptualization of identity and individual development found in Cisneros' work radically transforms both the Bildungsroman and the standard wisdom of developmental psychology. Carol Gilligan takes issue with the traditional "developmental litany" which "intones the celebration of separation, autonomy, individuation, and natural rights" (23). Gilligan cites Nancy Chodorow's claim for differences between female and male identity formation based on the child's recognition of similarity to (female) or difference from (male) the primary caretaker—most often maternal in our society—in order to examine both its empirical effects and its theoretical implications. Criticizing conventional notions that reduce development to a simple linear ordering based on separation, Gilligan instead envisions separation and attachment as a "reiterative counterpoint in human experience," recognizing both the "role of separation as it defines and empowers the self" and "the ongoing process of attachment that creates and sustains the human community" (156). She sees a mature stage of development as one in which the individual recognizes her interconnectedness with the world, achieving a balance between responsibility to herself and responsibility to others (155).

Cisneros' Esperanza explores the difficulties—and the possibilities—inherent in the struggle for such a balance, as she learns that neither self nor community can sustain itself independently; each requires the other. For example, when she senses the difficulty of reconciling "femininity" with conventional notions of adulthood, she determines "not to grow up tame like the others" and instead practices her "own quiet war," "leav[ing] the table *like a man*, without putting back the chair or picking up the plate" (82, emphasis mine). But this strategy of male emulation only shifts the burden to her mother (whose sacrifices are described in the segment which immediately follows), and casts herself into the role of the "bad" woman, the villainess in the movies "with red red lips who is beautiful and cruel." Esperanza admires the selfishness of this woman whose "power is her own. She will not give it away," yet when she tries to envision such an identity for herself, the callousness of such power brings her to an abrupt— and disturbing—realization (82). When "the three sisters"— her friends' *comadres*, whose eerie clairvoyance suggests both the Fates and Macbeth's witches—order her to make a wish, she complies, thinking "Well, why not?" But when she is immediately reprimanded, "When you leave you must remember to come back for the others," she feels chastised and guilty: "Then I didn't know what to say. It was as if she could read my mind, as if she knew what I had wished for, and I felt ashamed for having made such a selfish wish" (97).

The sisters recognize that Esperanza is "special," that "she'll go very far," and that she does therefore have a responsibility to herself and her talent, a responsibility which will necessitate her packing her "bags of books and paper." Esperanza likewise realizes the implications of her talents, acknowledging in her final vignette that she will indeed go far: "one day I will say goodbye to Mango. I am too strong for her to keep me here forever" (101). And yet her power and freedom are both circumscribed and expanded through being shared. She will never be like the "tame" women "who lay their necks on the threshold waiting for the ball and chain" (82); but neither will she be like Stephen Dedalus, who sees his art as a function of his own autonomy, necessitating his abandonment of home, fatherland, and church.[9] Esperanza senses her ongoing responsibility: not toward the centers of (relative) power, the fathers and husbands who contribute to the oppression of Mango Street's women by demanding obedience and docility, but toward those to whom Cisneros has dedicated the work: "*A las Mujeres.*" Her loyalty is toward the less powerful, the less strong, the less articulate in the dominant language: toward those, the sisters remind her, "who cannot leave as easily as you." Although she recognizes in her closing statement that her achievements might be misunderstood by friends and neighbors, she reassures herself that all will be rectified: "They will not know I have gone away to come back. For the ones I left behind. For the ones who cannot get out" (102). By the end of her narrative, then, Esperanza attains the balanced maturity described by Gilligan.

Notes

8. I use the term "American" as per standard academic usage, to designate canonical literature of the United States, but distance myself from such usage with quotation marks since in actuality the United States constitutes only a single aspect of the culture of the Americas, and the canon only one aspect of United States literature.

9. "I will tell you what I will do and what I will not do. I will not serve that in which I no longer believe whether it call itself my home, my fatherland or my church: and I will try to express myself in some mode of life or art as freely as I can and as wholly as I can, using for my defense the only arms I allow myself to use—silence, exile, and cunning" (Joyce 246–47).

ELLEN MCCRACKEN ON THE DEMYSTIFICATION OF PATRIARCHAL VIOLENCE

On the surface the compelling desire for a house of one's own appears individualistic rather than community oriented, but Cisneros socializes the motif of the house, showing it to be a basic human need left unsatisfied for many of the minority population under capitalism. It is precisely the lack of housing stability that motivates the image's centrality in works by writers like Cisneros and Rivera. For the migrant worker who has moved continuously because of job exigencies and who, like many others in the Chicano community, has been deprived of an adequate place to live because of the inequities of income distribution in U.S. society, the desire for a house is not a sign of individualistic acquisitiveness but rather represents the satisfaction of a basic human need. Cisneros begins her narrative with a description of the housing conditions the protagonist's family has experienced:

> We didn't always live on Mango Street. Before that we lived on Loomis on the third floor and before that we lived on Keeler. Before Keeler it was Paulina, and before that I can't remember. But what I remember most is moving a lot ...
> We had to leave the flat on Loomis quick. The water pipes broke and the landlord wouldn't fix them because the house was too old.... We were using the washroom next door and carrying water over in empty milk gallons.
>
> (p. 7)

Cisneros has socialized the motif of a house of one's own by showing its motivating roots to be the inadequate housing conditions in which she and others in her community lived. We learn that Esperanza, the protagonist Cisneros creates, was subjected to humiliation by her teachers because of her family's living conditions. "You live *there*?" a nun from her school had remarked when seeing Esperanza playing in front of the flat on

Loomis. "*There*. I had to look where she pointed—the third floor, the paint peeling, wooden bars Papa had nailed on the windows so we wouldn't fall out. You live *there*? The way she said it made me feel like nothing ..." (p. 9). Later, after the move to the house on Mango Street that is better but still unsatisfactory, the Sister Superior at her school responds to Esperanza's request to eat lunch in the cafeteria rather than returning home by apparently humiliating the child deliberately: "You don't live far, she says ... I bet I can see your house from my window. Which one? ... That one? she said pointing to a row of ugly 3-flats, the ones even the raggedy men are ashamed to go into. Yes, I nodded even though I knew that wasn't my house and started to cry ..." (p. 43). The Sister Superior is revealing her own prejudices; in effect, she is telling the child, "All you Mexicans must live in such buildings." It is in response to humiliations such as these that the autobiographical protagonist expresses her need for a house of her own. Rather than the mere desire to possess private property, Esperanza's wish for a house represents a positive objectification of the self, the chance to redress humiliation and establish a dignified sense of her own personhood.

TOMOKO KURIBAYASHI ON SPACE AND BILINGUALISM

Cisneros' narrative illuminates the linguistic, spatial and sexual oppression that racist society imposes on minority—more specifically Chicana—women, but also offers a somewhat hopeful perspective on future possibilities. Architecture is a central means by which society as well as Cisneros express and experience oppression as well as hope for change. In the beginning of Cisneros' novel, Esperanza yearns for acquisition of cultural ideals of the white society, most specifically the white, middle-class house widely displayed in mass media. Esperanza's architectural craving recreates the author Cisneros' childhood experiences in a Mexican-American ghetto in

Chicago. Cisneros recollects her family house, "crowded as the nine of us were in cramped apartments where there were children sleeping on the living room couch and fold-out Lazy Boy, and on beds set up in the middle room, where the only place with any privacy was the bathroom" ("Notebook" 69). She also remembers wondering "why our home wasn't all green lawn and white wood like the ones in 'Leave It To Beaver' or 'Father Knows Best'" (72).

These television programs played a significant role in aggravating the Chicana girl's sense of her family's architectural deficiency. Cisneros' narrator, Esperanza, also wants a house just like the ones she sees on television and all her family members share her dream:

> [My parents] always told us that one day we would move into a house, a real house that would be ours for always so we wouldn't have to move each year. And our house would have running water and pipes that worked. And inside it would have real stairs, not hallway stairs, but stairs inside like the houses on T.V. And we'd have a basement and at least three washrooms so when we took a bath we wouldn't have to tell everybody. Our house would be white with trees around it, a great big yard and grass growing without a fence. This was the house Papa talked about when he held a lottery ticket and this was the house Mama dreamed up in the stories she told us before we went to bed. (4)

Despite the parents' hopeful tone, it is unlikely that they will ever have such a house, as the narrative soon makes clear. When socioeconomic conditions render it so difficult—almost impossible—for Chicano/as to acquire such houses, mainstream culture's architectural ideal, which purportedly inspires cultural and economic aspirations in every viewer, only helps oppress the minority populations further.

Young Esperanza is keenly aware of how houses define and represent the resident's social status; so simply having a roof over one's head is not enough. Esperanza remembers how ashamed she felt when she pointed to a third-floor flat where she lived, to a nun from her school. The nun asked, "You live *there*? The way she said it made me feel like nothing. *There*. I lived *there*. I nodded" (5). She then resolved that she would have to have "a real house. One I could point to" (5), to be accepted into mainstream society. When her family moves to Mango Street, she still knows that the house is not respectable enough and yearns to escape to a better place.

But later her vision changes and she contemplates the possibility of housing the poor in her future house:

> People who live on hills sleep so close to the stars they forget those of us who live too much on earth. They don't look down at all except to be content to live on hills. They have nothing to do with last week's garbage or fear of rats. Night comes. Nothing wakes them but the wind.
>
> One day I'll own my own house, but I won't forget who I am or where I came from. Passing bums will ask, Can I come in? I'll offer them the attic, ask them to stay, because I know how it is to be without a house. (87)

Owning and controlling her own space is to own her self. One cannot become oneself without having one's own place. As Cherríe Moraga asserts, the "anti-materialist approach [that some white, middle-class feminists take] makes little sense in the lives of poor and Third World women" (129), when material conditions are so much a part of their oppression that coming into possession of material necessities is a must for becoming one's own person. But Esperanza does more than owning herself in the quoted passage. In other words, she does not unquestioningly embrace white, materialist beliefs in earthly possessions and financial security as a priority in and by themselves. First, Esperanza challenges mainstream society's definition of the family. Secondly, and more importantly, taking the socially rejected and oppressed—regardless of their gender, ethnicity, and other differences—into her own space is an expression of Esperanza's defiance of the dominant culture which bases itself on a rigid socioeconomic hierarchy and on dichotomous thinking. Her act turns the condition of exclusion of social outcasts into that of inclusion. Moreover, her gesture connects her future to her origin, her future self to Mango Street: "I won't forget who I am or where I came from" (21). Merging the public and the private, or the inside and the outside, is moving toward liberating women of her ethnic background as well as liberating any women who are confined indoors while men move much more freely outside houses. Once the distinction between the inside and the outside collapses, there is no more confining anybody indoors. Merging the two seemingly separate spaces, then, means doing away with rigid gender differentiations as well.

YVONNE YARBRO-BEJARANO ON CHICANA FEMINIST PERSPECTIVE

Writing is central in Sandra Cisneros' work of fiction *The House on Mango Street*.[10] *Mango St.* and Helena María Viramontes' collection of stories *Moths*,[11] are innovative in opposite directions—*Moths* characterized by formal experimentation, *Mango St.* by a deceptively simple, accessible style and structure. The short sections that make up this slim novel, *Mango St.*, are marvels of poetic language that capture a young girl's vision of herself and the world she lives in. Though young, Esperanza is painfully aware of the racial and economic oppression her community suffers, but it is the fate of the women in her barrio that has the most profound impact on her, especially as she begins to develop sexually and learns that the same fate might be hers. Esperanza gathers strength from the experiences of these women to reject the imposition of rigid gender roles predetermined for her by her culture. Her escape is linked in the text to education and above all to writing. Besides finding her path to self-definition through the women she sees victimized, Esperanza also has positive models who encourage her interest in studying and writing. At the end of the book, Esperanza's journey towards independence merges two central themes, that of writing and a house of her own: "a house as quiet as snow, a space for myself to go, clean as paper before the poem" (100).[12]

Esperanza's rejection of woman's place in the culture involves not only writing but leaving the barrio, raising problematic issues of changing class:

> I put it down on paper and then the ghost does not ache so much. I write it down and Mango says goodbye sometimes. She does not hold me with both arms. She sets me free. One day I will pack my bags of books and paper. One day I will say goodbye to Mango. I am too strong for her to keep me here forever. One day I will go away. Friends and neighbors will say, what happened to Esperanza? Where did she go with all those books and paper? Why did she march so far away? (101–02)

But Esperanza ends the book with the promise to return: "They will not know I have gone away to come back. For the ones I left behind. For the ones who cannot get out" (102).

The House on Mango St. captures the dialectic between self and community in Chicana writing. Esperanza finds her literary voice through her own cultural experience and that of other Chicanas. She seeks self-empowerment through writing, while recognizing her commitment to a community of Chicanas. Writing has been essential in connecting her with the power of women and her promise to pass down that power to other women is fulfilled by the writing and publication of the text itself.

Notes

10. *The House on Mango Street* (Houston: Arte Publico Press, 1985).

11. *The Moths and Other Stories* (Houston: Arte Publico Press, 1985).

12. Sonia Saldívar-Hull includes a discussion of *Mango St.* in "Shattering Silences: The Contemporary Chicana Writer," forthcoming in *Women and Words: Female Voices of Power and Poetry*, Ed. Beverly Stoelbe (University of Illinois Press).

If ideological and economic considerations structure Moraga's and Lizárraga's rape narratives, it is the theme of loss of innocence that predominates in Sandra Cisneros' short story "Red Clowns."[8] In this vignette we encounter Esperanza, the innocent and naive protagonist who is accompanying her older and street savvy friend Sally to the carnival. Sally disappears with her boyfriend and Esperanza, alone in the amusement park, is attacked by a group of boys. The narrative begins with the bitter recriminations of a disillusioned and traumatized Esperanza after the sexual transgression has occurred where, in a monologue full of hurt and despair, she mourns her loss of innocence: "Sally, you lied. It wasn't what you said at all. What he did. Where he touched me. I didn't want it, Sally. The way they said it, the way it's supposed to be, all the storybooks and movies, why did you lie to me?" (93). The diatribe is directed not only at Sally the silent interlocutor but at the community of women who keep the truth from the younger generation of women in a conspiracy of silence. The protagonist discovers a conspiracy of two forms of silence: silence in not denouncing the "real" facts of life about sex and its negative aspects in violent sexual encounters, and complicity in embroidering a fairy-tale-like mist around sex, and romanticizing and idealizing unrealistic sexual relations.

The protagonist confronts the hard truth and spits it out at what she perceives to be the perpetrators of the sex-is-glamorous myth:

> You're a liar. They all lied. All the books and magazines, everything that told it wrong. Only his dirty fingernails against my skin, only his sour smell again. The moon that watched. The tilt-a-whirl. The red clowns laughing their thick-tongue laugh. (94)

The theme of the silent, voiceless victim, the woman that is afraid to denounce her attackers, is reiterated in Cisneros' story: "Sally, make him stop. I couldn't make them go away. I couldn't do anything but cry. I don't remember. It was dark. I don't remember. I don't remember. Please don't make me tell it all" (93). This response to block out the rape scene and, to become silent and withdrawn is common in victims of sexual assault.[9]

Notes

8. "Red Clowns," in *The House on Mango Street* (Houston: Arte Publico Press, 1984).

9. See Elizabeth Ordóñez, "Sexual Politics and The Theme of Sexuality in Chicana Poetry," in *Women in Hispanic Literature: Icons and Fallen Idols*, Ed. Beth Miller (Berkeley: University of California Press, 1983), 316–39.

JULIÁN OLIVARES ON THE POETICS OF SPACE

I should like to discuss some of these stories and vignettes in order to demonstrate the manner in which Cisneros employs her imagery as a poetics of space and, while treating an "unpoetic" subject—as she says, expresses it poetically so that she conveys another element that Bachelard notes inherent to this space, the dialectic of inside and outside, that is, *here* and *there*, integration and alienation, comfort and anxiety (211–12). However, Cisneros again inverts Bachelard's pronouncement on the poetics of space; for Cisneros the inside, the *here*, can be confinement and a source of anguish and alienation. In this discussion we will note examples of (1) how Cisneros expresses an ideological perspective of the downtrodden but, primarily, the condition of the Hispanic woman; (2) the process of a girl's growing up; and (3) the formation of the writer who contrives a special house of her own. (...)

Mango Street is a street sign, a marker, that circumscribes the neighborhood to its Latino population of Puerto Ricans, Chicanos and Mexican immigrants. This house is not the young protagonist's dream house; it is only a temporary house. The semes that we ordinarily perceive in house, and the ones that Bachelard assumes—such as comfort, security, tranquility, esteem—are lacking. This is a house that constrains, one that she wants to leave; consequently, the house sets up a dialectic of inside and outside: of living *here* and wishing to leave for *there*.

The house becomes, essentially, the narrator's first universe. She begins here because it is the beginning of her conscious narrative reflection. She describes the house from the outside; this external depiction is a metonymical description and presentation of self: "I knew then I had to have a house. A real house. One I could point to." By pointing to this dilapidated house, she points to herself. House and narrator become identified as one, thereby revealing an ideological perspective of poverty and shame. Consequently, she wants to point to another house and to point to another self. And as she longs for this other house and self, she also longs for another name. But she will find that in growing up and writing, she will come to inhabit a special house and to fit into, find comfort, in her name.

In "My Name" the protagonist says: "In English my name means hope. In Spanish it means too many letters. It means sadness, it means waiting ... It is the Mexican records my father plays on Sunday mornings when he is shaving, songs like sobbing" (12). In this vignette Esperanza traces the reason for the discomfiture with her name to cultural oppression, the Mexican males' suppression of their women. Esperanza was named after her Mexican great-grandmother who was wild but tamed by her husband, so that: "She looked out the window all her life, the way so many women sit their sadness on an elbow ... Esperanza; I have inherited her name, but I don't want to inherit her place by the window" (12). Here we have not the space of contentment but of sadness, and a dialectic of inside/outside. The woman's place is one of domestic confinement, not one of liberation and choice. Thus, Esperanza would like to baptize herself "under a new name, a name more like the real me, the one nobody sees. Esperanza as Lisandra or Maritza or Zeze the X. Yes. Something like Zeze the X will do" (13). That is, Esperanza prefers a name not culturally embedded in a dominating, male-centered ideology.

Such a dialectic of inside/outside, of confinement and desire for the freedom of the outside world is expressed in various stories. Marin, from the story of the same name, who is too beautiful for her own good and will be sent back to Puerto Rico to her mother, who wants to work downtown because "you ... can meet someone in the subway who might marry and take you to live in a big house far away," never comes out of the house "until her aunt comes home from work, and even then she can only stay out in front. She is there every night with the radio ... Marin, under the streetlight, dancing by herself, is singing the same song somewhere. I know. Is waiting for a car to stop, a star to fall. Someone to change her life. Anybody" (27–8). And then there is Rafaela, too beautiful for her own good:

> On Tuesdays Rafaela's husband comes home late because that's the night he plays dominoes. And then Rafaela, who is still young, gets locked indoors because her husband is afraid Rafaela will run away since she is too beautiful to look at. ("Rafaela Who Drinks Coconut and Papaya juice on Tuesdays," 76)

One way to leave house and barrio is to acquire an education. In "Alicia Who Sees Mice" (32), a vignette both lyrical and hauntingly realistic, the narrator describes her friend's life. Alicia, whose mother has died so she has inherited her "mama's rolling pin and sleepiness," must arise early to make her father's lunchbox tortillas:

> Close your eyes and they'll go away her father says, or you're just imagining. And anyway, a woman's place is sleeping so she can wake up early with the tortilla star, the one that appears early just in time to rise and catch the hind legs hidden behind the sink, beneath the four-clawed tub, under the swollen floorboards nobody fixes in the corner of your eyes.

Here we note a space of misery and subjugation, a dialectic of inside/outside, a Latina's perception of life—all magnificently crystallized in the image of the "tortilla star." To Alicia Venus, the morning star, does not mean wishing upon or waiting for a star to fall down—as it does for Rafaela, nor romance nor the freedom of the outside world; instead, it means having to get up early, a rolling pin and tortillas. Here we do not see the tortilla as a symbol of cultural identity but as a symbol of a subjugating ideology, of sexual domination, of the imposition of a role that the young woman must assume. Here Venus—and the implication of sex and marriage as escape—is deromanticized, is eclipsed by a cultural reality that points to the drudgery of the inside. Alicia "studies for the first time at the university. Two trains and a bus, because she doesn't want to spend her whole life in a factory or behind a rolling pin ... Is afraid of nothing except four-legged fur and fathers."

Maria Szadziuk on Becoming a Woman in Bi-Ethnic Space

Such change does not happen in Cisneros's *Mango Street*, except in dreams, making this memoir in some ways more "realistic." Whereas Negi's cultural trajectory is far from typical for a first-generation immigrant, a second-generation immigrant could probably report an experience fairly similar to that of Esperanza, the narrator/protagonist of Cisneros's memoir. Born and educated in the United States, Esperanza is handicapped by her Hispanic background and the family's modest financial means. Having previously moved many times, when the family finally settles into the house on Mango Street, it seems their final dwelling as well as the limit of their mobility. The ghetto feeling in Cisneros's narrative is more pronounced than in Santiago's, since Esperanza's entire life is spent on Mango Street. The neighborhood-as-prison becomes a well-founded obsession and an echo of Negi's mobility can be found only in the initial fragment, where Esperanza remembers her past life as a series of different dwellings:

We didn't always live on Mango Street. Before that we lived on Loomis on the third floor, and before that we lived on Keeler. Before Keeler it was Paulina, and before that I can't remember. But what I remember most is moving a lot. Each time it seemed there'd be more of us. By the time we got to Mango Street we were six—Mama, Papa, Carlos, Kiki, my sister Nenny and me.

The house on Mango Street is ours and we don't have to pay rent to anybody or share the yard with the people downstairs or be careful not to make too much noise and there isn't a landlord banging on the ceiling with a broom.

But even so, it's not the house we'd thought we'd get.

(7)

Like Negi's disappointment with New York, the house on Mango Street is an ironic fulfillment of a dream, the family's long-expected permanent dwelling which by no means matches their expectations. As a child, Esperanza becomes painfully aware of the relationship between dwelling and social status, an awareness that initially stems from the shocked reaction of one of the nuns upon seeing the girl's house on Loomis Street. It is the outside world that sets a living standard and marginalizes those below it. Space available to a given ethnic group is restricted and determined by social status and income bracket. Mango Street's poor neighborhood, however, is both a ghetto and an ethnic haven. "All brown all around, we are safe," states the narrator; "But watch us drive into a neighborhood of another color and our knees go shakity-shake and our car windows get rolled up tight and our eyes look straight" (29).

In *Mango Street*, the conception of space is clearly related to the house, which denotes both the disappointing place where one lives and the place to which one hopes to move some day, both confinement and the desire to fly away, both temporary roof over one's head and the mythical space associated with writing, dreaming, expanding, loving and any form of personal fulfilment that provides a way out. The house literally defines a person, as suggested by Esperanza's continual reference to people in terms of "she lives upstairs" (14) or "the lady who owns the big building next door, three apartments front and back" (64). Suggesting that each person is confined within a closed space, the house is a sign of oppression, often imposed on the Hispanic woman, but also symbolizes the American Dream of a better life which includes the notion of a better house. The house thus repeats the pattern set by the neighborhood, being both a safe haven and a prison.

The limits imposed by the actual space and by the oppressive dominant culture are reflected in the outcome of any attempts to transcend them. In one vignette we are told about the little boy who "learned to fly and dropped from the sky like a sugar donut, just like a falling star, and exploded down to earth" (31). Another vignette tells of the girl who loved fun and boys only to end up "happily" in her own house, looking at the manicured ceiling all day and only occasionally beaten by her husband. In the case of Esperanza herself, the delights of a new position are soured because she is too shy to join the others during lunch breaks; despite her efforts to join the "special" schoolmates who are allowed to eat in "the canteen," she is left eating her rice sandwich alone and crying. Lost chances and thwarted attempts to communicate are a recurrent motif in *Mango Street*. Esperanza is unable to make her blind aunt see the pictures in her book, or to share her favorite poem with the half-witted neighbor girl; she cannot keep her friend who prefers being with boys, and she is unable to be nice to an elderly co-worker without being sexually abused. On top of her rejection by the society at large or Mango Street itself, she is doomed to being alone with her dreams since they do not fit the local standards.

Whereas in Santiago's text, Negi's traveling through real spaces inhabited by varying blends of the Puerto Rican and North American cultures is echoed by her resolute upward mobility, in Cisneros's narrative any real movement is prohibited and escape is present only as a desire to escape. Thus while travel between two cultural poles—one related to childhood, home, mother, family, emotional ties, and the other to adult life, society, school, intellectual achievement—is the common element in both these narratives, the way it is realized varies considerably. Negi is determined to succeed whatever the culture in which she is immersed, and her curiosity and ambition seem to produce the right mixture of a willingness to conform and an "onward and upward" drive. Although her success has a price in terms of cultural identity, it is a success nevertheless. Esperanza, in contrast, tends to contemplate rather than argue and dream rather than move. Social mobility in *Mango Street* is more a desire than a fact, and in her essentially static world, it is only the protagonist's mind that travels.

LESLIE PETTY ON THE "DUAL"-ING IMAGES OF LA MALINCHE AND LA VIRGIN DE GUADALUPE

The work of a Chicana writer is threatened in a different way by the la Malinche archetype, a way that makes the role model of la Virgen de Guadalupe just as dangerous. For Cisneros, the dilemma is creating a role model for herself and other Chicanas that is neither limited by this good/bad duality ingrained in Mexican culture, nor too "Anglicized" (Rodriguez-Aranda 65) to adequately represent their experience. When interviewing Cisneros, Pilar E. Rodriguez-Aranda observes, "the in-between is not ours.... So if you want to get out of these two roles, you feel you're betraying you're [sic] people" (65). In response to this dilemma, Cisneros claims that she and other Chicana women must learn the art of "revising" themselves by learning to "accept [their] culture, but not without adapting [themselves] as women" (66).

The House on Mango Street is just such an adaptation. The author "revises" the significance of the Chicana archetypes of la Malinche and la Virgen de Guadalupe through her characterization of females in the book. By recasting these mythical stories from the female perspective, Cisneros shows how artificial and confining these cultural stereotypes are, and through her creation of Esperanza, imagines a protagonist who can embody both the violation associated with la Malinche and the nurturing associated with la Virgen de Guadalupe, all the while rejecting the feminine passivity that is promoted by both role models. Therefore, Esperanza transcends the good/bad dichotomy associated with these archetypes and becomes a new model for Chicana womanhood: an independent, autonomous artist whose house is of the heart, not of the worshiper, nor of the conqueror.

Maria Elena de Valdés observes that in *The House on Mango Street*, Esperanza is "drawn to the women and girls [in the story] as would-be role models" (59). Not surprisingly, Esperanza does not find many lives that she would like to emulate. Her rejection of these role models stems from each character's close alliance with one of the two Mexican archetypes. Cisneros shows how being culturally defined by either of these two roles makes for an incomplete, frustrated life. While the Virgin Mother is a venerated role model, Cisneros complicates this veneration through her characterization of other maternal figures, most notably, Esperanza's mother and her aunt, Lupe.

In "Hairs," Cisneros paints an intimate picture of Esperanza's relationship with her mother, whose hair holds "the smell when she makes room for you on her side of the bed still warm with her skin, and you sleep near her" (6). Like the Virgin, Esperanza's mother is a protector, a haven for her daughter during the rain. This idealized memory is marred somewhat in "A Smart Cookie," in which it is clear that Esperanza's mother is very talented, that she can "speak two languages" (90), and "can sing an opera" (90), but that she is not contented with her life. Mother says, "I could've been somebody, you know?" (91). Apparently, being the nurturing, self-sacrificing mother whose hair "smells like bread" is not sufficient to make Esperanza's mother's life complete. Instead of being a dependent female, Esperanza's mother tells her daughter that she has "[g]ot to take care all your own" (91), alluding to a culture that desires virgin-like women, but which does not reward the desired passivity with the care and adoration also reserved for the Virgin; instead, Mother mentions several friends who have fulfilled their roles as mothers but have consequently been left alone. Mother encourages her daughter to reject this self-sacrificing path that Mexican culture sees as noble, like the Virgin, and to choose instead to "study hard" (91) in school in order to prepare herself for independence.

A more forceful rejection of the Virgin archetype is evident in the characterization of Esperanza's aunt, Guadalupe. Like the mythic character for whom she is named, Aunt Lupe is a passive woman in a shrine, but in "Born Bad," this connection is corrupted with images of sickness, stagnation, and helplessness. Unlike Paz's assertion that "through suffering, our women become like our men: invulnerable, impassive and stoic" (30), there is nothing idyllic or positive about Cisneros's portrayal of a suffering woman. Instead of living in a resplendent holy place, Cisneros's Guadalupe lives in a cramped, filthy room with "dirty dishes in the sink" (60), and "ceilings dusty with flies" (60). The passivity of Lupe is the result of a debilitating illness that has caused her bones to go "limp as worms" (58). Guadalupe is chaste[7] like the Virgin, but her lack of sexual activity is not a sign of her moral superiority; it is again caused by her illness and associated with the frustration and longing of "the husband who wanted a wife again" (61).

Aunt Lupe, like Esperanza's mother, does provide a haven of sorts for the young protagonist, even though Esperanza "hate[s] to go there alone" (60). Esperanza says that she likes her aunt because "she listen[s] to every book, every poem I ever read her" (60). Aunt Lupe's home gives Esperanza a safe place to explore her passion for writing and her aspirations as a poet, and this protection is the most positive connection that Cisneros makes between Aunt Lupe and the Virgin. Aunt Lupe encourages Esperanza to "keep writing" because "[i]t will keep [her] free" (61). Ironically, the life that Aunt Lupe encourages Esperanza to follow is not one of passivity and self-sacrifice associated with the Holy Mother; instead Lupe gives Esperanza a push towards independence much like the one that the adolescent girl receives from her own mother. After Aunt Lupe dies, Esperanza begins to "dream the dreams" (61) of pursuing her education and her artistic aspirations.

Note

7. While "chaste" is often used to designate virginity, *The American Heritage College Dictionary* lists "celibacy" as a third definition. While Lupe is obviously not virginal, all signs indicate that she is currently, and permanently, celibate.

JACQUELINE DOYLE ON PERSONAL SPACE

Pondering the doors shut by the male custodian of the library, Woolf in 1928 "thought how unpleasant it is to be locked out; and ... how it is worse perhaps to be locked in" (*A Room* 24). To be confined within male structures might be as great a disadvantage to the female artist as to be outside them. To achieve the "freedom and fullness of expression" Woolf considered necessary to art, women must design new spaces appropriate to their dreams and needs. "A book is not made of sentences laid end to end," wrote Woolf, "but of sentences built ... into arcades or domes. And this shape too has been made by men out of their own needs for their own uses" (80).

As Esperanza shapes her narrative, images of constricting, infelicitous space are balanced by powerful feminine images of what Bachelard terms "felicitous space." Their third-floor flat on Loomis above the boarded-up laundromat, which they had to leave "quick" when the water pipes broke, is an early source of shame to Esperanza, when the nun from her school says "'You live *there*?' ... You live *there*? The way she said it made me feel like nothing" (5). The series of third-floor flats, on Loomis, and before that on Keeler, and before that on Paulina, more flats than Esperanza can remember, would not seem to exemplify Bachelard's intuition that "life begins well, it begins enclosed, protected, all warm in the bosom of the house" (7). What Esperanza "remember[s] most is moving a lot" (3). "I never had a house," she complains to Alicia on Mango Street, "... only one I dream of" (107). Yet the "maternal features of the house" that Bachelard describes are literally exemplified in the felicitous peace of Esperanza's mother's body, "when she makes a little room for you on her side of the bed still warm with her skin, and you sleep near her," "when she is holding you, holding you and you feel safe" (6). Within this shelter, the small girl can begin to dream.

The overcrowded house on Mango Street, with its "swollen" door, "crumbling" bricks, and "windows so small you'd think they were holding their breath," is "not the house we'd thought we'd get," Esperanza complains, "not the way they told it at all" (3–4). Yet Mango Street becomes an integral part of herself, the source of her art and her freedom. *Las comadres*, the three magical sisters, tell Esperanza: "When you leave you must remember to come back for the others. A circle, understand? You will always be Esperanza. You will always be Mango Street. You can't erase what you know: You can't forget who you are" (105). If Mango Street is "not the way they told it at all," then Esperanza's developing resolve is to remember herself through a new telling that will not erase realities, and to begin by circling back to "what I remember most ... Mango Street, sad red house, the house I belong but do not belong to" (110). Bachelard suggests that circular structures "help us to collect ourselves, permit us to confer an initial constitution on ourselves," and advises that "by remembering 'houses' and 'rooms,' we learn to 'abide' within ourselves" (234, xxxiii). Esperanza's negotiation with her origins is more ambivalent and less nostalgic than Bachelard's, but remembering Mango Street is nevertheless intimately connected to the formation of her identity as a woman, an adult member of her community, and a writer.

Through Mango Street, Esperanza is able to explore the tensions between belonging and not belonging. Hers is a story, she tells us, "about a girl who didn't want to belong" (109). In "My Name" she confides her rebellious desire to "baptize myself under a new name, a name more like the real me, the one nobody sees. Esperanza as Lisandra or Maritza or Zeze the X. Yes. Something like Zeze the X will do" (11). Her successive baptisms, like the names for the shape-shifting clouds in "And Some More," keep Esperanza's identity fluid. Yet she also acknowledges that the name Esperanza belongs to her, a legacy from her great-grandmother, a "wild horse of a woman." "I have inherited her name," Esperanza tells us, "but I don't want to inherit her place by the window" (11). When Alicia tells her that "like it or not" she is Mango Street and will come back, she replies:

> Not me. Not until somebody makes it better.
> Who's going to do it? The mayor?
> And the thought of the mayor coming to Mango Street makes me laugh out loud.
> Who's going to do it? Not the mayor. (107)

Through naming herself and her community, Esperanza returns both to accept and to alter her inheritance. Her most conspicuous alliances when she constitutes herself as speaking subject are ethnic and local. The "we" she speaks is Hispanic, herself and her barrio neighbors.[17] "Those who don't know any better come into our neighborhood scared," she says of outsiders:

> But we aren't afraid. We know the guy with the crooked eye is Davey the Baby's brother, and the tall one next to him in the straw brim, that's Rosa's Eddie V. and the big one that looks like a dumb grown man, he's Fat Boy, though he's not fat anymore nor a boy. (28)

Note

17. María C. Lugones and Elizabeth V. Spelman explore "the difference among women and how these differences are silenced" through a dialogue. The Hispana in the dialogue reflects on the different contexts in which she uses the word "we." In the paper, "when I say 'we' I am referring to Hispanas," she writes; 'you' refers to "the white/Anglo women that I address." However, she adds, " 'we' and 'you' do not capture my relation to other no-white women," and in a footnote she meditates on her general use of "we" outside of the paper: "I must note that when I think this "we," I think it in Spanish—and in Spanish this 'we' is gendered, 'nosotras.' I also use 'nosotros' lovingly and with ease and in it I include all members of 'La raza cosmica' (Spanish-speaking people of the Americas, la gente de colores: people of many colors). In the US, I use 'we' contextually with varying degrees of discomfort: 'we' in the house,

'we' in the department, 'we' in the classroom, 'we' in the meeting. The discomfort springs from the sense of community in the 'we' and the varying degrees of lack of community in the context in which the 'we' is used" ("Have We Got a Theory" 575). Although *The House on Mango Street* is clearly a feminist text, Esperanza does not use "we" to refer to women; instead "we" refers to herself and her family, herself and her childhood girlfriends, and herself and her neighborhood ethnic community ("brown allaround").

Works By Sandra Cisneros

Bad Boys, 1980.

The House on Mango Street, 1983.

"Los Tejanos: Testimony to the Silenced," 1984.

"An Interview with Ana Castillo," 1984.

"Bread, Dreams and Poetry: Luis Omar Salinas, the Man," 1984.

"Salvador Late or Early," 1986.

"Cactus Flowers: In Search of Tejana Feminist Poetry," 1986.

My Wicked Wicked Ways, 1987.

"Ghosts and Voices: Writing from Obsession," 1987.

"Notes to a Young(er) Writer," 1987.

"Do You Know Me? I Wrote The House on Mango Street," 1987.

Woman Hollering Creek and Other Stories, 1991.

Loose Woman: Poems, 1994.

"Guadalupe the Sex Goddess," 1996.

Hairs/Pelitos, 1997.

Caramelo, 2002.

Annotated Bibliography

Cisneros, Sandra. "Do You Know Me?: I Wrote The House on Mango Street." *The Americas Review* XV:1 (Spring 1987): pp. 77–79.

In this short article, Cisneros relates the process by which *The House on Mango Street* came to fruition.

Cruz, Felicia J. "On the Simplicity of Sandra Cisneros's *House on Mango Street*." *Modern Fiction Studies* 47:4 (Winter 2001): pp. 910–945.

In this essay, Cruz suggests that the readings of *The House on Mango Street* have exaggerated the simplicity of the text. She contends that the text and its relative depth depend upon the cultural cache, agenda, education and experience of the reader. Much of her analysis uses Terry Eagleton's *Literary Theory: An Introduction* as a lens through which one might question the rhetoric of the book.

Doyle, Jacqueline. "More Room of Her Own: Sandra Cisneros's *The House on Mango Street*." MELUS 19:4 (1994): pp. 5–35.

In this article, Doyle explores the ways in which Cisneros complicates Virginia Woolf's notion of "a room of one's own." Doyle pays particular attention to the effect of ethnicity on this "feminist inheritance."

Ganz, Robin. "Sandra Cisneros: Border Crossings and Beyond." *MELUS* 19:1 (Spring 1994): pp. 19–29.

Ganz provides basic background information on the author, linking her autobiographical experiences to the creation of Esperanza and her world and world views in *The House on Mango Street*.

Gutiérrez-Jones, Leslie S. "Different Voices: The Re-Building of the Barrio in Sandra Cisneros' *The House of Mango Street*." *Anxious Power: Reading, Writing, and Ambivalence in*

Narrative by Women. Eds. Carol J. Singley and Susan Elizabeth Sweeney. Albany: State University of New York Press, 1993: pp. 295–312

In this essay, Gutiérrez-Jones discusses the way in which Cisneros manipulates the bildungsroman form to suit the needs of a female, bi-ethnic narrator and author. Because both the author and her protagonist need to find space and freedom outside the cultural constraints of the barrio and white patriarchal culture, they need to shift the form so as not to become trapped again in the language and traditions of the oppressor.

Herrera-Sobek, María. "The Politics of Rape: Sexual Transgression in Chicana Fiction." *Chicana Creativity and Criticism: New Frontiers in American Literature, 2nd Ed.* Eds. María Herrera-Sobek and Helena María Viramontes. Albuquerque: University of New Mexico Press, 1996: pp. 245–256.

Herrera-Sobek examines rape as a metaphor in the work of Chicana writers, emphasizing that the metaphor is doubly powerful coming from the perspective of the twice marginalized Chicano female. The lens through which it is viewed is feminist which reinforces the idea that rape becomes the physical manifestation of patriarchal or phallocentric society. She posits that the metaphor is used to reject the oppression of women on multiple levels, from the broadest societal norms to the familial and individual. She asserts that the difference between Chicana fiction and that of other feminist writers utilizing the metaphor stems from the communal context in which the Chicana writers place the incidents.

Kuribayashi, Tomoko. "The Chicana Girl Writes Her Way In and Out: Space and Bilingualism in Sandra Cisneros' *The House on Mango Street.*" *Creating Safe Spaces: Violence and Women's Writings.* Eds. Tomoko Kuribayashi and Julie Tharpe. Albany: State University of New York Press: 1998. pp. 165–177.

In this article, Kuribayashi places protagonist, Esperanza, into three categories of marginalization: she is bi-ethnic, female and poverty-stricken. Because of these identities, Esperanza is forced to find new spaces to inhabit as the patriarchal culture from which she springs keeps her from having power as a woman, the house that she inhabits keeps her from having the social power of the signified wealthy, and her ethnic identity will prohibit her from mainstreaming into white middle America. She overcomes these problems by integrating her identities, using the spaces between English and Spanish to create a Utopian vision wherein she can acquire wealth but use it to better the lives of the people in the barrio, particularly the disenfranchised like the women around her and the homeless.

Matchie, Thomas. "Literary Continuity in Sandra Cisneros's *The House on Mango Street*." *The Midwest Quarterly* 37:1 (Autumn 1995): pp. 67–79.

Matchie suggests that Cisneros' *The House on Mango Street* fits as the third novel in Edgar Branch's notion of "literary continuity" which begins with Mark Twain's *The Adventures of Huckleberry Finn* and Salinger's *The Catcher in the Rye*. Like her predecessors, Cisneros writes a coming of age novel of a young protagonist profoundly affected by cultural norms. In terms of linguistic technique and use of archetype, Matchie suggests that this novel, though it is told by a young Chicano female, still fits into this American literary tradition.

McCracken, Ellen. "Sandra Cisneros' *The House on Mango Street*: Community-Oriented Introspection and the Demystification of Patriarchal Violence." *Breaking Boundaries: Latina Writing and Critical Readings*. Eds. Asunción Horno-Delgado, Eliana Ortega, Nina M. Scott and Nancy Saporta Sternbach. Amherst: The University of Massachusetts Press, 1989: pp. 62–71.

McCracken discusses the way in which Cisneros complicates the traditional male-oriented vision of the Bildungsroman in multiple ways, first giving a female perspective, second giving it a Chicana communal perspective, and third redefining its linguistic and ideological traditions. McCracken gives particular emphasis to the question of whether the book will be able to make its way into the literary canon without the current vogue of the highly individualistic search for self that defines those texts of the same genre. She questions whether the academy will embrace the idea of a communal creation of self, with particular attention paid to the collective creation of female identity within community spaces.

Norton, Jody. "History, Rememory, Transformation: Actualizing Literary Value." *The Centennial Review* 38:3 (Fall 1994): pp. 589–602.

In this article, Norton examines the idea John Ellis espouses: "[T]exts are made into literature by the community, not by the authors." Norton examines the way in which readers interact with and engage Esperanza and the literary text as an act of mutual identity formation.

Olivares, Julián. "Sandra Cisneros' *House on Mango Street* and the Poetics of Space." *Chicana Creativity and Criticism: New Frontiers in American Literature, 2nd Ed.* Eds. María Herrera-Sobek and Helena María Viramontes. Albuquerque: University of New Mexico Press, 1996: pp. 233–244.

Olivares explores the notion of space and the way in which Cisneros plays with Gaston Bachelard's idea of *The Poetics of Space*. Cisneros also treats the metaphor of poetics of space but in so doing she revisions one of its primary tenants, "the dialectic of the inside and outside" changing the inside from a place of inclusion to a space of subjugation particularly for Chicana women.

Petty, Leslie. "The 'Dual'-ing images of la Malinche and la Virgen de Guadalupe in Cisneros's *The House on Mango Street*." *MELUS* 25:2 (Summer 2000): pp. 119–132.

Petty examines the effect of two archetypal female representations, la Malinche and la Virgen de Guadalupe, in Cisneros's *The House on Mango Street*. She discusses the cultural importance of the Virgin and the Whore to the Mexican culture and the way in which it manifests itself in the novel.

Poey, Delia. "Coming of Age in the Curriculum: *The House on Mango Street* and *Bless Me, Ultima* as Representative Texts." *The Americas Review* 24:3/4 (Fall/Winter 1996): pp. 201–217.

Poey attempts to answer some of the culture war questions raised by E.D. Hirsch and Allan Bloom in the 1980's regarding multiculturalism in the educational system. She seeks to define what is meant by multiculturalism and to show the ways in which these texts interact with the established traditions of the canon and the communities they seek to represent.

Santz, Martha. "Returning to One's House: An Interview with Sandra Cisneros." *Southwest Review* 82:2 (Spring 1997): pp. 166–85.

Satz conducted two interviews, one in 1985 and one in 1996 with Sandra Cisneros. In them, she questions Cisneros on the origins of *The House on Mango Street* and the evolution of themes throughout her work, paying particular attention to ethnicity and gender issues.

Scalise Sugiyama, Michelle. "Of Woman Bondage: The Eroticism of Feet in *The House on Mango Street*." *The Midwest Quarterly* 41:1 (Autumn 1999): pp. 9–20.

Scalise Sugiyama explores the eroticism of feet and shoes as a metaphor for men's exertion of control over women. She cites multiple ways in which the feet and their adornment reinforce the patriarchal power structure and traces that theme throughout the book as a larger metaphor.

Szadziuk, Maria. "Culture as Transition: Becoming a Woman in Bi-Ethnic Space." *Mosaic* 32:3 (September 1999): pp. 109–129.

Szadziuk explores, via three Chicano writers, the notion of "culture-in-transition" and the way in which each of the authors treats the idea within their autobiographical works. She asks specifically what the effect of distance from the dominant culture (first/second/third generation) has had on the narrative techniques and modes of the texts in question.

De Valdés, Maria Elena. "In Search of Identity in Cisneros's *The House on Mango Street.*" *Canadian Review of American Studies* 23:1 (Fall 1992): pp. 55–72.

De Valdes writes about the connection that must occur between the speaking protagonist and the protagonist in actuality. She argues that Esperanza must be her speech; it acts as a continuation and manifestation of the self, based on observation both within and without. She integrates into the argument recognition of the marginalization of the character based on her feminist inclinations and Chicana heritage.

Yarbro-Bejarano, Yvonne. "Chicana Literature from a Chicana Feminist Perspective." *Chicana Creativity and Criticism: New Frontiers in American Literature, 2nd Ed.* Eds. María Herrera-Sobek and Helena María Viramontes. Albuquerque: University of New Mexico Press, 1996. pp. 213–219.

In this essay, Yarbro-Bejarano explains the distinct nature of the Chicana Feminist perspective as it differs from that of white Feminism and the Chicana perspective. She emphasizes the idea that Chicana feminism is born of the neighborhoods, barrios and streets within which these women live and work. As a result, the search for self in this type of literature necessarily recognizes the community and its part of freeing/enslaving the self. This point of view also critically integrates communal history in the United States, paying particular attention to racism and sexism within the community as well as without. She utilizes the works of particular Chicana writers to establish both the history of the perspective and its manifestations in the literature.

Contributors

Harold Bloom is Sterling Professor of the Humanities at Yale University and Henry W. and Albert A. Berg Professor of English at the New York University Graduate School. He is the author of over 20 books, including *Shelley's Mythmaking* (1959), *The Visionary Company* (1961), *Blake's Apocalypse* (1963), *Yeats* (1970), *A Map of Misreading* (1975), *Kabbalah and Criticism* (1975), *Agon: Toward a Theory of Revisionism* (1982), *The American Religion* (1992), *The Western Canon* (1994), and *Omens of Millennium: The Gnosis of Angels, Dreams, and Resurrection* (1996). *The Anxiety of Influence* (1973) sets forth Professor Bloom's provocative theory of the literary relationships between the great writers and their predecessors. His most recent books include *Shakespeare: The Invention of the Human* (1998), a 1998 National Book Award finalist, *How to Read and Why* (2000), *Genius: A Mosaic of One Hundred Exemplary Creative Minds* (2002), and *Hamlet: Poem Unlimited* (2003). In 1999, Professor Bloom received the prestigious American Academy of Arts and Letters Gold Medal for Criticism, and in 2002 he received the Catalonia International Prize.

Camille-Yvette Welsch is an instructor of writing at the Pennsylvania State University. Her work has appeared in *Calyx* and *Red Cedar Review*.

The late **Jody Norton** taught Women's Studies and English at Eastern Michigan University for seven years and authored "Transchildren and the Discipline of Children's Literature" and "Bodies That Don't Matter: The Discursive Effacement of Sexual Difference."

Maria Elena de Valdés is the editor of *Approaches to Teaching Garcia Marquez's* One Hundred Years of Solitude and *The Shattered Mirror: Representations of Women in Mexican Literature*.

Thomas Matchie is a Professor of English at North Dakota State University. He received the Victor J. Emmett Award for the best essay of the year in the publication "The Midwest Quarterly." He is the author of several articles on Native American and regional authors.

Michelle Scalise Sugiyama is an Assistant Professor of English at the University of Oregon. She is the author of "On the Origins of Narrative: Storytellers Bias as a Fitness-Enhancing Strategy."

Leslie S. Gutiérrez-Jones was a PhD candidate at Cornell University in 1993. Her dissertation was entitled "Through the I of a Child: Personal Politics in the Kunstlerroman of the Marginalized Woman."

Ellen McCracken is a Professor in the Department of Spanish and Portuguese at University of California, Santa Barbara. She is the author of *From* Mademoiselle *to* Ms.*: Decoding Women's Magazines, New Latina Narrative: The Feminine Space in Postmodern Ethnicity* and *Fray Angélico Chávez: Poet, Priest, Artist.*

Tomoko Kuribayashi teaches at University of Wisconsin, Stevens Point. She is the co-editor of *Creating Safe Space: Violence and Women's Writing* and is currently co-editing *The Outsider Within: Ten Essays on Modern Japanese Women Writers.*

Yvonne Yarbro-Bejarano is a Professor in the Department of Spanish & Portuguese at Stanford University. She is the author of *Feminism and the Honor Plays of Lope de Vega, The Wounded Heart: Writing on Cherríe Moraga,* and co-editor *of Chicano Art: Resistance and Affirmation.*

María Herrera-Sobek is the Chair of the Chicano Studies Department at the University of California, Santa Barbara where she holds the Luis Leal Endowed Chair in Chicano Studies. She is the author of several works including *The Bracero Experience: Elitelore versus Folklore* and *Northward Bound: The Mexican Immigrant Experience in Ballad and Song*.

Julián Olivares is a Professor of Modern and Classical Languages at the University of Houston. He worked as an editor at Arte Publico Press. His work includes a book entitled *Cuentos Hispanos de los Estados Unidos*.

Maria Szadziuk is a doctoral candidate in Romance Studies at Cornell University. She is also a certified translator of multiple languages.

Leslie Petty is a doctoral candidate in English at the University of Georgia. Her work has appeared in *Southern Quarterly* and *MELUS*. She is a recipient of the Carrie Chapman Catt Prize for Research on Women and Politics in 2001.

Jacqueline Doyle is a professor of English as well as a graduate student advisor at the California State University, Hayward.

Acknowledgments

"History, Rememory, Transformation: Actualizing Literary Value" by Jody Norton: pp. 594–596. This work originally appeared in *The Centennial Review* 38:3 (Fall 1994), published by Michigan State University Press. Reprinted by permission.

"In Search of Identity in Cisneros's *The House on Mango Street*" by Maria Elena De Valdés. From *Canadian Review of American Studies* 23:1 (Fall 1992): pp. 61–63. © 1992 by Maria Elena De Valdés. Reprinted by permission of the University of Toronto Press Incorporated.

"Literary Continuity in Sandra Cisneros's *The House on Mango Street*" by Thomas Matchie. From *The Midwest Quarterly* 37:1 (Autumn 1995): pp. 74–76. © 1995 by Thomas Matchie. Reprinted by permission.

"Of Woman Bondage: The Eroticism of Feet in *The House on Mango Street*" by Michelle Scalise Sugiyama. From *The Midwest Quarterly* 41:1 (Autumn 1999): pp. 11–13. © 1999 by Michelle Scalise Sugiyama. Reprinted by permission.

Gutiérrez-Jones, Leslie S. "Different Voices: The Re-Building of the Barrio in Sandra Cisneros' *The House on Mango Street*": pp. 300–303. Reprinted by permission from *Anxious Power: Reading, Writing, and Ambivalence in Narrative by Women*, eds. Carol J. Singley and Susan Elizabeth Sweeney, the State University of New York Press. © 1993 by the State University of New York. All rights reserved.

McCracken, Ellen. *Sandra Cisneros'* The House on Mango Street*: Community-Oriented Introspection and the Demystification of Patriarchal Violence*: pp. 64–65. © 1989 by The University of Massachusetts Press. Reprinted by permission.

"The Chicana Girl Writes Her Way In and Out: Space and Bilingualism in Sandra Cisneros' *The House on Mango Street*" by Tomoko Kuribayashi. From *Creating Safe Spaces: Violence and Women's Writings*: pp. 166–167. Eds. Tomoko

Index